# NARROWING THE DEVELOPMENT GAP

## FOLLOW-UP MONITOR OF THE ASEAN FRAMEWORK FOR EQUITABLE ECONOMIC DEVELOPMENT

MAY 2023

ASIAN DEVELOPMENT BANK

ADB

# CONTENTS

# TABLES, FIGURES, AND BOXES

## Tables

## Figures

## Boxes

# FOREWORD FROM ADB

The Asian Development Bank (ADB) and the Association of Southeast Asian Nations (ASEAN) share a commitment to integration, sustainable development, and inclusion. This has spanned a wide range of cooperation in areas including project financing, policy dialogue, capacity building, information sharing, and joint production of knowledge products. ASEAN economies have remained resilient through the coronavirus disease pandemic, but continued vigilance will be needed to ensure future development progress.

It is often said that one should measure what matters. This report, *Narrowing the Development Gap: Follow-Up Monitor of the ASEAN Framework for Equitable Economic Development,* takes this advice to heart and undertakes regular monitoring of ASEAN's development gaps. It focuses on a selective and balanced set of indicators providing simple yet comprehensive preparation on the economic, social, and environmental dimensions of well-being.

In this study, we aim to (i) develop a monitoring system to track the historical progress of a balanced set of indicators on equitable development that is consistent with the desired characteristics and targets of the ASEAN Economic Community, the ASEAN Socio-Cultural Community, and the Sustainable Development Goals monitored under the 2030 Agenda for Sustainable Development of the United Nations; and (ii) create linkages with monitoring initiatives already being pursued by ASEAN to ensure sustainability of this exercise.

The research benefited from the guidance of the Initiative for ASEAN Integration Task Force and the perceptive inputs from colleagues in the ASEAN Secretariat and ADB. We look forward to ADB's continued partnership with ASEAN and rest assured we are committed to support the region's recovery efforts.

Stronger regional cooperation will be needed to help build a resilient ASEAN and to ensure that no part of the ASEAN community is left behind.

**Ahmed M. Saeed**
Vice-President for East Asia, Southeast Asia, and the Pacific
Asian Development Bank

# FOREWORD FROM ASEAN

The ASEAN Framework for Equitable Economic Development is an important initiative of the Association of Southeast Asian Nations (ASEAN) that emphasises equitable economic development for the region. Aimed at narrowing the development gaps both within and between the ASEAN member states, the framework focuses on providing better access to opportunities for human development, social welfare and justice, as well as ensuring more inclusive participation in ASEAN integration process and community building efforts.

A study to monitor the ASEAN Framework for Equitable Economic Development was conducted in 2014 to track indicators across two broad sets of development outcomes and policies, namely: economic development and human development. Taking into consideration the rapid and evolving development at the global and regional levels, particularly the significant impact of the COVID-19 pandemic, there was a need for ASEAN to undertake a follow-up study to assess the recent performance of ASEAN member states in selected indicators and to identify to what extent of development gaps have narrowed in the region.

This important study focuses on a more selective and balanced set of indicators to capture the economic, social, and environmental dimensions of well-being in the region. It attempts to identify how development gaps within and between ASEAN member states could be further narrowed and reinforces ASEAN's commitment to promote equitable economic growth in the region, and the steps needed to ensure that this commitment remains a top priority.

In this regard, I would like to congratulate the Initiative for ASEAN Integration Task Force for elevating this initiative as one of the priority economic deliverables under Cambodia's ASEAN Chairmanship in 2022. I would also like to commend the dedicated research team of the Asian Development Bank for putting so much effort into producing this publication to make it really useful and meaningful. Their collective efforts have resulted in a thorough and thoughtful analysis of the status of equitable economic development in ASEAN.

I am confident that this publication will serve as a useful and insightful resource to promote sustainable economic growth in the region and inspire new ideas for future actions in order to realise a sustainable, inclusive and resilient ASEAN Community for all.

**Kao Kim Hourn**
Secretary-General
ASEAN

# ACKNOWLEDGMENTS

The research was supported by the regional technical assistance on Policy Advice for COVID-19 Economic Recovery in Southeast Asia (TA 9964). The team from the Regional Cooperation and Operations Coordination Division, Southeast Asia Department of the Asian Development Bank (ADB) led by James Villafuerte, principal economist, with support from Dulce Zara, senior regional cooperation officer and Georginia Nepomuceno, regional cooperation and integration consultant, managed the study and coordinated the preparation of this publication under the supervision of Alfredo Perdiguero, director, Regional Cooperation and Operations Coordination Division. Melissa May Ebarvia extended administrative support.

Jose Ramon Albert, international statistics consultant prepared the report in close consultation with the ASEAN Secretariat. The publication is gratefully acknowledging the guidance and endorsement of the Initiative for ASEAN Integration Task Force comprising of the Permanent Representatives of the 10 ASEAN member states. The Initiative for ASEAN Integration and Narrowing the Development Gap Division coordinated inputs from relevant units of the ASEAN Secretariat, including from the Monitoring Surveillance and Coordination Division, Statistics Division, Analysis and Monitoring on Finance and Socio-Economic Issues Division of the ASEAN Economic Community Department, and the Monitoring Division of the ASEAN Socio-Cultural Community Department.

Very thoughtful insights were provided by ADB colleagues, including from the Economic Research and Regional Cooperation Department: Abdul Abiad, director of Macroeconomics Research Division; Elaine Tan, advisor and head of Statistics and Data Innovation Unit; and Sanchita Basu Das, economist at the Regional Cooperation and Integration Division; from the Sustainable Development and Climate Change Department: Oleksiy Ivaschenko, senior social protection and jobs specialist and Flordeliza Huelgas, social protection consultant, Social Development Thematic Group; and from the Lao People's Democratic Republic Resident Mission of Southeast Asia Department: Emma Allen, senior country economist and Soulinthone Leuangkhamsing, senior economics officer.

Effective 1 February 2021, ADB placed a temporary hold on sovereign project disbursements and new contracts in Myanmar. The bank continues to monitor the situation in the country. Information on Myanmar in this report are from international sources and/or arising from attempts to accurately assess aggregate Cambodia, the Lao People's Democratic Republic, Myanmar, and Viet Nam performance to meet the objectives of the study.

Lawrence Casiraya edited the manuscript. Mike Cortes typeset and produced the layout as well as created the cover design. Maria Guia de Guzman proofread the report. The Knowledge Support Division of ADB's Department of Communications facilitated the publishing of this report.

# ABBREVIATIONS

ADB         Asian Development Bank
AEC         ASEAN Economic Community
AFEED       ASEAN Framework for Equitable Economic Development
ASCC        ASEAN Socio-Cultural Community
ASEAN       Association of Southeast Asian Nations
ASEAN-6     Association of Southeast Asian Nations comprising Brunei Darussalam, Indonesia, Malaysia,
            the Philippines, Singapore, and Thailand
CLMV        Cambodia, the Lao People's Democratic Republic, Myanmar, and Viet Nam
COVID-19    coronavirus disease
CV          coefficient of variation
GDP         gross domestic product
GMM         generalized method of moments
GPI         Gender Parity Index
HDI         Human Development Index
IAI         Initiative for ASEAN Integration
ICT         information and communication technology
LAO PDR     Lao People's Democratic Republic
NEET        not in employment, education, or training
SDG         Sustainable Development Goal
PPP         purchasing power parity
UNDP        United Nations Development Programme
UNESCO      United Nations Educational, Scientific and Cultural Organization
WEF         World Economic Forum

# EXECUTIVE SUMMARY

- Regular monitoring of progress in narrowing the development gap is critical to ensure that Association of Southeast Asian Nations (ASEAN) programs remain impactful and relevant. This report builds on the first monitor of the ASEAN Framework for Equitable Economic Development (AFEED) produced in 2014. The AFEED covered a wide number of indicators, most of which were economic indicators, where data could readily be provided by the World Bank. This second AFEED monitor focuses on a more selective and balanced set of indicators, comprising a total of 39 indicators from 12 dimensions that have the advantage of being simple yet comprehensive, adequately capturing the different economic, social, capability, and environmental dimensions of well-being. The choice of dimensions and indicators examined in this monitor are underpinned by the following principles:

  (i) **The dimensions and indicators of well-being are based on frameworks that are relevant to all ASEAN member states.** Apart from aligning with the desired characteristics of the ASEAN Economic Community and ASEAN Socio-Cultural Community, the dimensions and indicators shall be consistent with indicators adopted in global accords such as the Sustainable Development Goals.

  (ii) **The indicators are widely accepted, readily available, and credible.** Previous ASEAN reports have stressed the need for indicators to be (i) relevant; (ii) consistent or coherent in terms of concepts and definitions, methods, coverage, and timeliness; (iii) credible in terms of data source; and (iv) complete in terms of country coverage.

  (iii) **The monitoring process must be sustainable.** This will mean leveraging existing mechanisms that are already in place, with room to expand in the future as statistical capacities improve.

- This second AFEED monitor provides a simple and concise snapshot of development progress in ASEAN as whole, and across ASEAN member states based on the indicator framework. Most indicators examined, however, only cover 2000 to 2019, due to data availability. Thus, this report does not cover the extent of the development progress and trajectory that has changed in the ASEAN due to the coronavirus disease pandemic. Convergence analysis is also undertaken in this report to determine if the ASEAN community has been successful in narrowing development gaps.

- Over the years, ASEAN has transformed into the world's fifth-largest economy. In 2000–2021, ASEAN's gross domestic product has grown at a rate of 4.6% per year, contracting only in 2020 by 3.6% from the previous year amid the onset of the COVID-19 pandemic. ASEAN also accounts for about 8.5% of the world's population as of 2021. The ASEAN community has made progress in various socioeconomic fronts, but at different paces for member states. The pandemic, however, pushed back progress in the region by several years. Member states will need to find pathways for accelerated growth, and the entire ASEAN community will need to ensure that that development gaps are reduced.

**Overall human development**: Human development in the ASEAN community, as reflected by the Human Development Index, has improved over time, and the gap among ASEAN member states has also narrowed.

**Material well-being (income and poverty)**. Upward income convergence was also being achieved before 2020, with the ratio of the gross domestic product per capita of ASEAN-6, the first six members of ASEAN (Brunei Darussalam, Indonesia, Malaysia, the Philippines, Singapore, and Thailand) to the four newer member states Cambodia, the Lao People's Democratic Republic (Lao PDR), Myanmar, and Viet Nam (CLMV), declining from 3.4 in 2000 to 2.1 in 2019, and further to 2.0 in 2020—with a slight divergence for 2021 with the ratio rising to 2.1. Growth comparison between ASEAN-6 and CLMV shows a reversal between pre-pandemic and post-pandemic periods. In the pre-pandemic years, CLMV was growing much faster on average than ASEAN-6. But the growth of CLMV dropped sharply in the wake of the pandemic. The region's rapid economic growth in the last 2 decades had contributed to the significant reductions in poverty. The proportion of ASEAN people living in extreme poverty, i.e., below the international poverty line of $2.15 per person per day, reduced to less than one in 30 persons (3.3%) in 2019, from about one in three persons (36.6%) in 2000.

**Employment and working conditions**. Unemployment rates have been increasing in all ASEAN member states. The rise of unemployment in member states is higher among females than males in Brunei Darussalam, Malaysia, and Viet Nam; lower for females in Indonesia and the Philippines; and the same for both sexes in Singapore and Thailand. Across economies, the youth aged 15 to 24 has a much larger unemployment rate than adults aged 25 and over.

**Access to finance**. The region has also been successful in increasing access to finance, although the proportion of adults with an account at a formal financial institution remains less than half in Cambodia (33%), the Lao PDR (37%), and Myanmar (48%).

**Health and nutrition**. Maternal deaths have declined from about 200 deaths per 100,000 live births in 2000–2004 to about half, i.e., 107 deaths in 2015–2019. This is a result of increased proportion of births attended by skilled health personnel across member states.

**Education**. Literacy and participation rates have also been increasing with investments in schooling and other learning environments. Pandemic-induced school closures have, however, had repercussions to providing access to school participation, and to quality learning for all, the latter of which has been a challenge even in pre-pandemic times in most of CLMV and the Philippines. Skills development, which is crucial for the economic recovery, has also been uneven in the region.

**Digital access and skills**. Internet penetration and the coverage by at least 4G mobile network have both risen in the region, but more so in ASEAN-6 than in CLMV. Internet penetration averages 63% among ASEAN member states as of 2020—an increase of about 55.7 percentage points from 2000. Nearly all member states provide more than 80% coverage by at least 4G mobile network. Digital divides, however, persist in infrastructure and in skills. Recent data on digital skills suggests a wide disparity in information and communication technology skills across ASEAN member states, in favor of richer member states— Brunei Darussalam, Malaysia, and Singapore.

**Gender equality**. In nearly all ASEAN member states, females and males are at par in youth literacy rate with the gender parity index for 2019 data averaging to 1.00. Women leadership across all ASEAN member states, however, is far from parity with men. Among ASEAN member states, only the Philippines has managed to stay consistently in the top 20 rankings in the Global Gender Gap Index released by the World Economic Forum.

**Living conditions**. Access to electricity is nearing universal in the ASEAN community, with nearly all but two member states providing access to more than 95% of their respective populations, as of the latest data. The only exceptions are Cambodia (86.4%) and Myanmar (70.4%), which, however, have considerably increased access to electricity from 2000 to 2020.

**Social safety nets**. Coverage of social insurance ranges between 1.9% (in Cambodia) to 15.2% (in Viet Nam). Malaysia and Thailand also have about three out of every four persons benefiting from social assistance, but coverages of social assistance in Cambodia, Myanmar, and Viet Nam is only about one-fifth or less of the respective populations. Data on coverage for labor market programs is limited, with only two ASEAN member states having at least two data points.

**Environment and climate change**. Much work is needed to ensure environmental protection in the region. None of the ASEAN members have reached targets to conserve at least 10% of coastal and marine areas as of 2021.

**Governance**. Higher-income countries such as Brunei Darussalam, Malaysia, and Singapore tend to get high performance marks in various metrics on governance, while low-income countries such as Cambodia, the Lao PDR, and Myanmar tend to do poorly.

# I.    BACKGROUND

In 1967, the governments of Indonesia, Malaysia, the Philippines, Singapore, and Thailand established the Association of Southeast Asian Nations (ASEAN) by virtue of the ASEAN Declaration (Bangkok Declaration).[1] ASEAN was formed with a common vision of accelerated, sustained, and broad-based economic growth; social progress in Southeast Asia, and cultural development, aside from the promotion of peace and security in the region. Brunei Darussalam subsequently joined ASEAN in 1984, followed by Viet Nam in 1995, the Lao People's Democratic Republic (Lao PDR) and Myanmar in 1997, and Cambodia in 1999.

In this report, the socioeconomic conditions in the 10 ASEAN member states are sometimes examined in terms of trends in ASEAN-6—i.e., the first six members of ASEAN (Brunei Darussalam, Indonesia, Malaysia, the Philippines, Singapore, and Thailand), relative to the four newer member states Cambodia, the Lao PDR, Myanmar, and Viet Nam (CLMV). The ASEAN-6 has had better starting conditions relative to CLMV, and one of the concerns in the ASEAN community is to narrow the development gaps across members states, not only in terms of average per capita income but also in terms of human resources, institutional capacity, the state of infrastructure, and the level of competitiveness.

Thus, the Initiative for ASEAN Integration (IAI) was launched at the Fourth ASEAN Informal Summit in Singapore in 2000 to serve as a framework for regional cooperation through which the more developed ASEAN member states could help the others most in need, to narrow the development gap, and enhance ASEAN's competitiveness as a region. In 2001, the strategy for the implementation of the IAI was refined to focus on CLMV through the Ha Noi Declaration. Since then, four IAI work plans for 2002–2008, 2009–2015, 2016–2020, and 2021–2025 have laid down measures and actions for ASEAN-6 to help CLMV, supported by ASEAN partners and international organizations. The most recent work plan—the IAI Work Plan IV (2021–2025)—was adopted at the 37th ASEAN Summit in November 2020. It maintains the five strategic areas of the IAI Work Plan III[2] aside from considering new challenges and emerging crosscutting issues (ASEAN 2020f). These crosscutting issues include Industry 4.0, gender and social inclusion, environmental sustainability, and the impact of the coronavirus disease (COVID-19) pandemic.

Over the years, the ASEAN has transformed into the world's fifth-largest economy (with a total combined gross domestic product [GDP] of 10 ASEAN member states valued at $3.1 trillion as of 2021). The ASEAN community is poised to become the fourth-largest economic bloc in the world by 2030 (ASEAN 2021a). Aside from having a rapidly growing share of the world's output, ASEAN also accounts for about 8.5% of the world's population as of 2021. In 2000–2021, ASEAN's GDP grew at a rate of 4.6% per year, contracting only in 2020 by 3.6% from the previous year amid the onset of the COVID-19 pandemic (Figure 1). Further, the total population in the region has grown from 524.5 million in 2000 to 674.5 million in 2021. CLMV's share of the population in the region has been around 12%, while the share of CLMV output to that of ASEAN is at 3.7% in 2021, an increase from 2.2% in 2000.

---

[1]    ASEAN. The Founding of ASEAN.

[2]    The five areas are food and agriculture; trade facilitation; micro, small, and medium-sized enterprises; education; and health and well-being.

**Figure 1: Gross Domestic Product and Population across ASEAN-6 and Cambodia, the Lao People's Democratic Republic, Myanmar, and Viet Nam, 2000–2021**

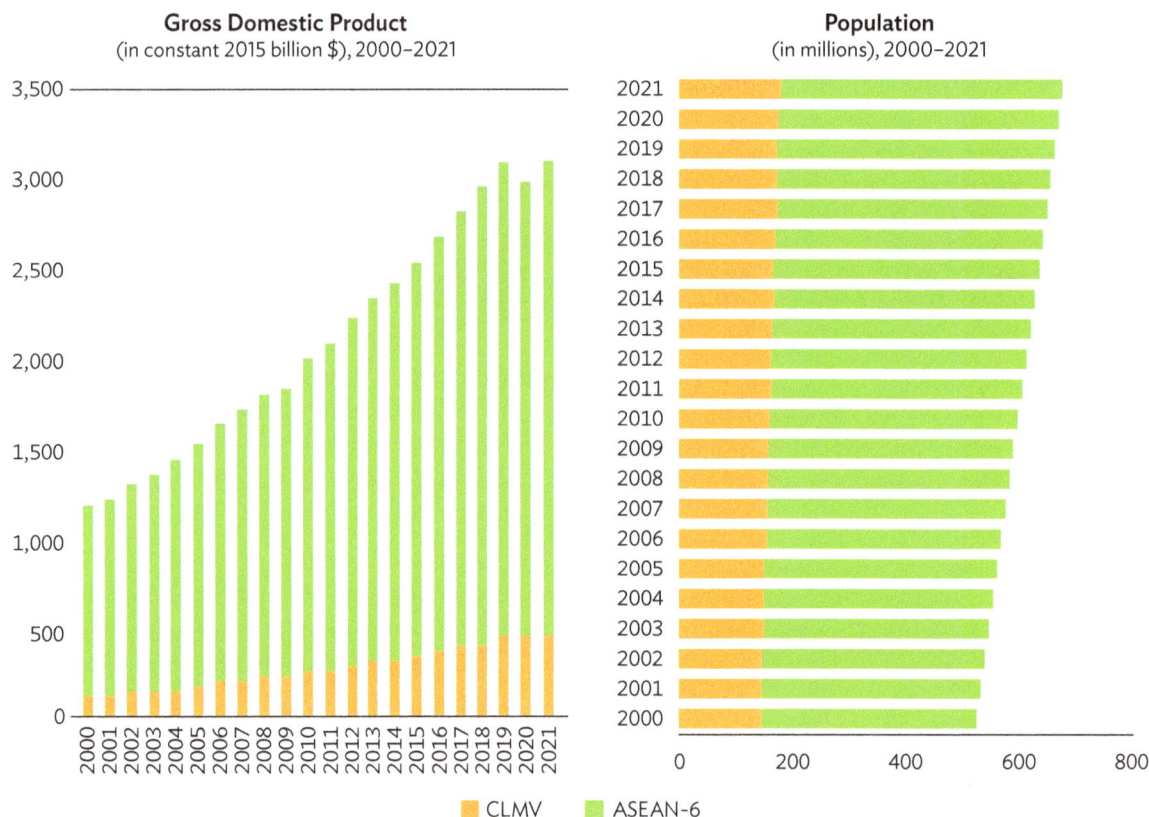

**Gross Domestic Product**
(in constant 2015 billion $), 2000–2021

**Population**
(in millions), 2000–2021

CLMV    ASEAN-6

ASEAN-6 = Association of Southeast Asian Nations comprising Brunei Darussalam, Indonesia, Malaysia, the Philippines, Singapore, and Thailand.
Sources: World Bank. World Bank Open Data. https://data.worldbank.org/ (accessed 21 August 2022); United Nations Department of Economic and Social Affairs Population Division. 2022. *World Population Prospects 2022*. https://population.un.org/wpp/ (accessed 21 August 2022).

Collectively and individually, ASEAN member states have been making headway in reducing extreme poverty prior to the pandemic. From 2000 to 2019, the proportion of the populations living on less than $2.15 per day in member states have reduced by as much as 8.3% per year (in the Lao PDR) to 76.1% annually (in Myanmar). Malaysia (2013) and Thailand (2015) have reached the zero extreme poverty target ahead of the 2030 end year for the Sustainable Development Goals (SDGs). Recent data before the pandemic puts the proportion in extreme poverty at less than 5% in six of the seven members for which comparable poverty estimates are available. The only exception is the Lao PDR, where 7.1% of the population live on less than $2.15 per day as of 2018, and 32.5% have incomes below $3.65 per day (Figure 2).

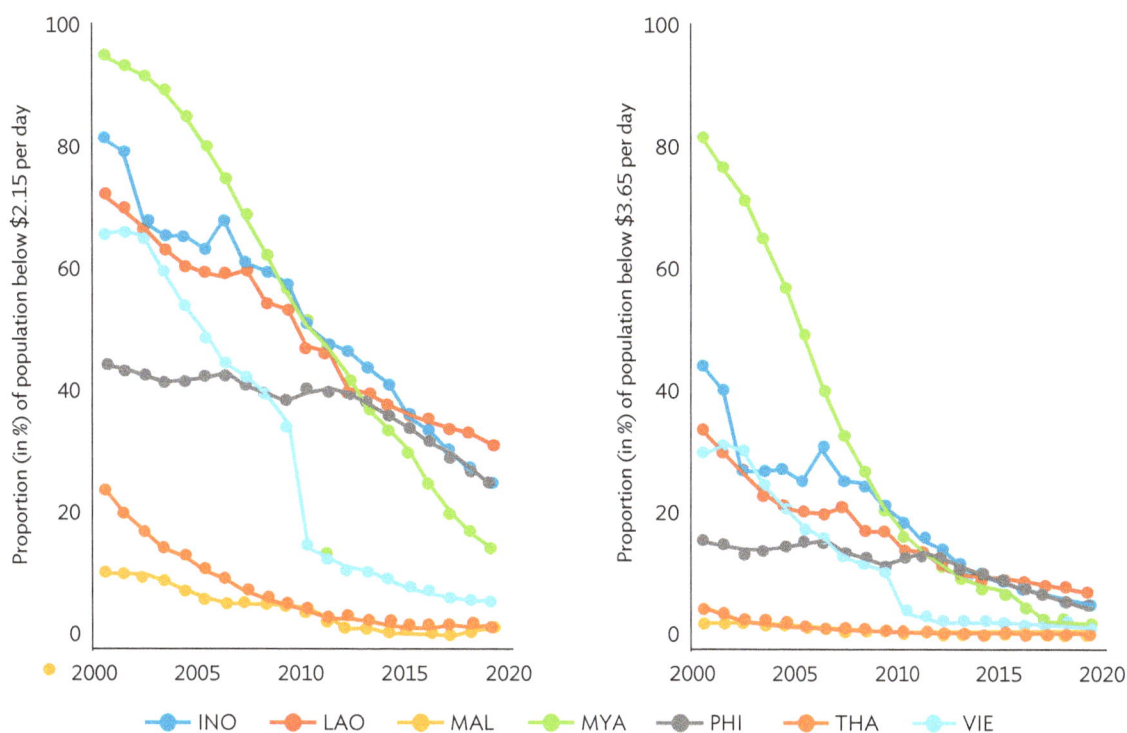

**Figure 2: Proportion of Population in ASEAN Member States Living on Less Than $2.15 and $3.65 per Day (in purchasing power parity 2017 prices), 2000–2019**

ASEAN = Association of Southeast Asian Nations, INO = Indonesia, LAO = Lao People's Democratic Republic, MAL = Malaysia, MYA = Myanmar, PHI = Philippines, THA = Thailand, VIE = Viet Nam.
Note: While Cambodia monitors poverty, the World Bank has not generated poverty rates using international poverty lines for Cambodia.
Source: World Bank. 2022. Poverty and Inequality Platform. World Bank Group. https://pip.worldbank.org/home (accessed 8 January 2023).

The substantial reductions in poverty observed in ASEAN member states have been a result of rapid economic growth, but poverty reduction and economic growth have not always been accompanied by reduced income inequalities. The Gini coefficient[3] for expenditures (or incomes), which measures inequality, has been displaying various patterns across member states over time. Since 2000, latest data for ASEAN member states show that five—Malaysia, Myanmar, the Philippines, Thailand, and Viet Nam—have reduced their respective Gini coefficient compared to earliest years' data, implying that growth over the period went along with greater equality in the distribution of incomes (or expenditures) (Figure 3). However, the reverse case has been observed in Indonesia and the Lao PDR, with the distribution of income and spending becoming relatively more unequal over time. The poverty–income growth–inequality nexus has been rather complex. Poverty reduces with higher growth and reduced inequality. The persistently high levels of inequality in the Philippines and the rising inequality in

---

[3]    The Gini coefficient measures the extent to which income (or expenditure) distribution deviates from a perfectly equal distribution. A Lorenz curve plots the cumulative percentages of income received against the cumulative number of recipients, starting with the poorest individual. The Gini index measures the area between the Lorenz curve and a hypothetical line of perfect equality, expressed as a percentage of the maximum area under the line. The Gini ranges from zero (which reflects complete equality, i.e., all persons have the same income) to one (which indicates complete inequality, where one person has all the income while all others have none). While a larger Gini coefficient signifies more inequality, the interpretation of the Gini is more straightforward when the figures are compared across time and space.

Indonesia and the Lao PDR have reduced the extent to which economic growth benefited poor people in these countries. Therefore, the rates of extreme poverty reduction in Indonesia, the Lao PDR, and the Philippines have been slower than those in Myanmar and Viet Nam.

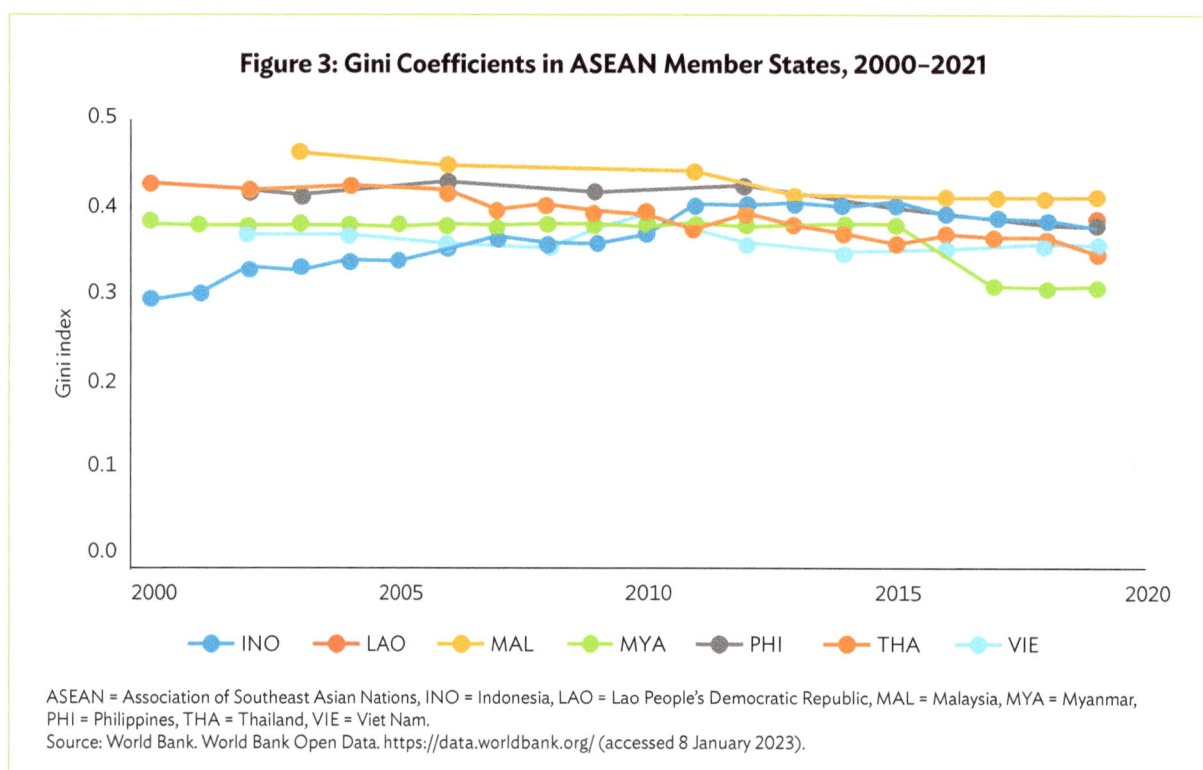

**Figure 3: Gini Coefficients in ASEAN Member States, 2000–2021**

ASEAN = Association of Southeast Asian Nations, INO = Indonesia, LAO = Lao People's Democratic Republic, MAL = Malaysia, MYA = Myanmar, PHI = Philippines, THA = Thailand, VIE = Viet Nam.
Source: World Bank. World Bank Open Data. https://data.worldbank.org/ (accessed 8 January 2023).

Aside from reduced poverty, ASEAN has made some progress in realizing decent work for all men and women, building skills of human capital, and improving the enabling environment for further growth and development, while having challenges in protecting the environment. The achievements in its development trajectory have been considerably affected by the pandemic. In 2020, however, because of containment measures to manage the spread of the virus (including lockdowns and restrictions in mobility and social interaction), unemployment rates have soared across the region. Lockdowns were estimated to have impacted especially informal workers. Informal workers are among those most vulnerable to disruption and income losses from the reduced economic activities, especially as they are often excluded from national social protection coverage (ASEAN 2020c, ASEAN 2020d, ASEAN 2020e). Economic recovery has gained momentum, albeit under a context of fragility, owing to weak demand for currencies in the region relative to the United States dollar aside from inflationary pressures, food, and energy insecurity due to the Russian invasion of Ukraine (ASEAN 2022b). The challenge is for the region to double down in progress and get back on its development path prior to the pandemic, and for the ASEAN community to narrow the development gap within the region.

Several ASEAN members, such as Cambodia, Indonesia, and the Philippines have been implementing large-scale conditional cash transfer programs targeted for poor families, to provide assistance and incentivize them to invest in the education and health of their family members. These social protection programs have significantly increased enrollment and attendance of children (Ryu 2021, Cahyadi et al. 2020, Ferreira et al. 2016) though effects on other outcomes such as learning achievements or later earnings have been mixed, depending on the social context. While the actual cash support provided to beneficiaries for these programs is small, i.e., they will not make poor households cross the poverty line, had these social protection programs not been in place amid the pandemic, undoubtedly, poverty in these countries would have become far more severe (Albert et al. 2022).

Using lessons from these social assistance programs, many countries in ASEAN have resorted to fiscal stimulus packages that included the provision to households of cash support, subsidies (for electricity or social security contributions), or opportunities to defer loan payments amid the onset and impact of the pandemic on jobs, income, and welfare. For instance, in 2020, the Philippines allocated around $3.9 billion for cash subsidies to 18 million low-income households over 2 months. Other more affluent ASEAN member states provided support for practically all citizens. In Singapore, citizens aged 21 and above were given about $640 each, while self-employed persons were paid around $2,116 in three tranches to supplement their incomes. In Indonesia and Viet Nam, "rice ATMs" were introduced while, in Thailand, pay-forward food coupons were provided.

Despite development gains in ASEAN, cross-country disparities in socioeconomic development outcomes remain a major challenge for the region (ASEAN 2021a; Asian Development Bank [ADB] and ASEAN Secretariat 2019; United Nations Ecoomic and Social Commission for Asia and the Pacific [UNESCAP] 2018a, 2018b, and 2010; Bunnag, 2019; Menon 2013). Narrowing the development gap across and within member states has been a key aspiration of the ASEAN community, which was formally established in 2015. Directions for the ASEAN community since the idea of its formation have been articulated in the blueprints for its three pillars— the ASEAN Political-Security Community Blueprint, the ASEAN Economic Community (AEC) Blueprint, and the ASEAN Socio-Cultural Community (ASCC) Blueprint—aside from the IAI Work Plan IV and the Master Plan for ASEAN Connectivity 2025. Regular monitoring of progress in regional integration and in narrowing the development gap is critical to ensure that programs in the ASEAN community remain impactful and relevant. The IAI workplan is the key instrument developed by the ASEAN for less-developed members to catch up with their more developed counterparts. Thus, ASEAN has in place several mechanisms to monitor progress in regional integration, including the ASEAN Community Progress Monitoring System (ASEAN 2017) and midterm reviews of the AEC Blueprint (ASEAN 2021b),[4] the ASCC Blueprint (ASEAN 2020a), and the Master Plan on ASEAN Connectivity 2025 (ASEAN 2020b).

Further, in 2014, ASEAN developed the ASEAN Framework for Equitable Economic Development (AFEED) monitor titled *Bridging the Development Gap: ASEAN Equitable Development Monitor 2014* (World Bank 2014). The AFEED monitor used a series of pre-identified indicators that were approved during the ASEAN Senior Economic Officials Meeting in 2014. The monitor tracks indicators across two broad sets of development outcomes and policies: (i) economic development (encompassing economic growth and macroeconomic stability, enterprise development, business regulation and facilitation, and access to finance); and (ii) human development (encompassing education, health, nutrition, water sanitation, and electricity).

In 2019, ASEAN proceeded with a similar initiative under the ambit of the IAI Task Force. In collaboration with ADB, the ASEAN Secretariat conducted a study, the *Assessment of the Progress in Narrowing Development Gap in ASEAN*. The study measured progress in narrowing the development gap in ASEAN, in particular, between the ASEAN-6 and CLMV. The study tracked the levels and trends of a series of selected indicators on economic and social development, and an index was computed by using various indicators for each category under economic development and social development. Under economic development, the study measured macroeconomic stability, infrastructure development, financial development, and institutional development of each ASEAN member state across different periods. The same methodology was applied in measuring social development by looking at progress in poverty reduction, and selected indicators of education, health, and nutrition. The study suggested that further assessment on narrowing the development gap and measurement on the performance of each ASEAN member state should be based on development thresholds or indicators that go beyond income levels.

---

4   The ASEAN Economic Community (AEC) 2025 is an "aspiration held by the 10 member states of ASEAN to be, by year 2025, (i) a highly integrated and cohesive economy; (ii) a competitive, innovative, and dynamic ASEAN; with (iii) enhanced connectivity and sectoral cooperation; (iv) by remaining resilient, inclusive, people-oriented, and people-centered and becoming a (v) global ASEAN."

The indicators and dimensions examined in this report (as well as supporting indicators) were chosen on the basis of their conceptual relevance to the ASEAN community Vision 2025 and their data availability. Development data are typically sourced from censuses, sample surveys, administrative data, and their frequency of reporting varies across countries. The GDP and other statistics on the national income accounts are compiled from several data sources. Because of the wide interest in measuring economic performance, GDP is reported most frequently among development indicators, at least on an annual basis (and often, quarterly data are also generated by national statistical systems). Sample surveys on household income or expenditure are the source of poverty data, but the frequency of conduct of these surveys, when they are done in countries, varies considerably. Some member states, such as Indonesia and Thailand (since 2006), conduct these poverty surveys every year, although most member states conduct these surveys every 3 to 5 years. Two member states, Brunei Darussalam and Singapore, do not monitor poverty.

Upon request of the IAI Task Force and the ASEAN Secretariat, ADB prepared a concept note that outlined the guiding principles for a follow-up monitor of the AFEED and described five existing frameworks for measuring well-being.[5] After a consultative process, ADB adopted a more straightforward objective and methodology to conduct a follow-up monitor of the AFEED, which is the subject of this report. This report describes the collective and individual historical progress of ASEAN across select dimensions of well-being and development indicators.

(A) **Dimensions of well-being.** The report adopts an eclectic approach combining the measures of well-being elaborated in existing regional and global frameworks.[6] Twelve main dimensions of economic and sociocultural well-being have been selected for study: (1) overall human development, (2) material well-being (income and poverty), (3) employment and working conditions, (4) access to finance, (5) health and nutrition, (6) education, (7) digital access and skills, (8) gender equality, (9) living conditions, (10) social safety nets, (11) environment and climate change, and (12) governance.

(B) **Development indicators.** The first AFEED Monitor (World Bank 2014) covered a wide number of indicators, most of which were economic indicators where data could readily be provided by the World Bank. This report focuses on a more selective and balanced set of 39 indicators from 12 dimensions of well-being. The intent is to focus on indicators that have the advantage of being simple yet comprehensive, adequately capturing the different economic, social, capability, and environmental dimensions of well-being. Moreover, the report prioritizes indicators that are currently included in the ASEAN Community Progress Monitoring System; the ASEANStats Database; the ASEAN Baseline Report on SDGs; the Medium-Term Reviews of the AEC and the ASCC; and the Master Plan on ASEAN Connectivity. Choosing indicators from these sources offers a couple of advantages. These indicators have gone through the formal process of review and endorsement by ASEAN member states. Further, both the ASEAN Secretariat and national statistical offices of ASEAN member states would already be collecting data on these indicators on a regular basis, as part of monitoring progress under the AEC and ASCC pillars and the SDGs. Where necessary, the report includes indicators that are not currently included in existing ASEAN publications or databases, but for which reliable and comparable data are available either from national statistical offices or reputable regional or global databases. The dimensions and indicators examined in this second AFEED Monitor are as follows (Table 1):

---

[5]    These were the OECD's *Better Life Initiatives*, the United Nations Development Programme's (UNDP's) *Human Development Index*, the ADB Institute's *Dimensions and Indicators of Quality of Life*, Malaysia's *Wellbeing Index*, and the UN's *Sustainable Development Goals*.

[6]    These frameworks include (i) the Sustainable Development Goals (SDGs); (ii) UNDP's Human Development Index (HDI); (iii) the Dimensions and Indicators of Quality of Life by the ADB Institute; (iv) the Framework for Inclusive Growth Indicators by ADB; (v) the Social Progress Index by the Social Progress Imperative; and (vi) the multidimensional poverty measures developed separately by the UNDP and the World Bank.

**Table 1: Dimensions and Indicators**

| Dimensions | Development Indicators |
|---|---|
| Overall human development | 1. Human Development Index |
| Material well-being (income and poverty) | 2. Gross domestic product per capita (in constant 2015 purchasing power parity [PPP] $)<br>3. Proportion of population below the international poverty lines ($2.15, $3.65, and $6.85 per person per day in 2017 PPP prices) |
| Employment and working conditions | 4. Unemployment rate<br>5. Proportion of informal employment in nonagricultural employment (by gender)<br>6. Proportion of youth (aged 15–24) not in education, employment, or training |
| Access to finance | 7. Commercial bank branches (per 100,000 adults)<br>8. Number of ATMs per 100,000 adults<br>9. Number of registered mobile money accounts per 1,000 adults<br>10. Proportion of adult population with account at formal financial institution |
| Health and nutrition | 11. Maternal mortality ratio<br>12. Proportion of births attended by skilled health personnel (%)<br>13. Under-5 mortality rate<br>14. Prevalence of stunting, height-for-age (% of children under 5) |
| Education | 15. Proportion of population aged 15 years and above achieving at least a fixed level of proficiency in functional literacy skill (%)<br>16. Adult literacy rate (aged 15 and over)<br>17. Youth literacy rate (aged 15–24)<br>18. Net enrollment rate (by education level); (tertiary levels are gross rather than net enrollment rates) |
| Digital access and skills | 19. Individuals using the internet (% of population)<br>20. Proportion of population covered by at least 4G mobile network<br>21. Proportion of youth and adults with information and communication technology skills, by type of skill (%) |
| Gender equality | 22. Literacy rate, Gender Parity Index (GPI)<br>23. School enrollment, GPI (by education level)<br>24. Global Gender Gap Index<br>25. Proportion of seats held by women in national parliaments (%)<br>26. Proportion of women in managerial positions (%) |
| Living conditions | 27. Proportion of urban population (in %) living in slums, informal settlements, or inadequate housing facilities<br>28. Access of population to safely managed drinking water services (%)<br>29. Access of population to safely managed sanitation services (%)<br>30. Access of population to electricity (%) |
| Social safety nets | 31. Proportion of population covered by social assistance programs (%)<br>32. Proportion of population covered by social insurance programs (%)<br>33. Proportion of population covered by labor market programs (%) |
| Environment and climate change | 34. Number of deaths, missing persons, and directly affected persons attributed to climate-related disasters per 100,000 population<br>35. Ratio of protected area to total area and forest cover to total land area<br>36. Coverage of protected areas in relation to marine areas |
| Governance | 37. Government Effectiveness Index<br>38. Business Climate Change Index – Ease of doing business score (0 = lowest performance to 100 = best performance)<br>39. Global Competitiveness Index |

Source: Consultations with the Initiative for ASEAN Integration Task Force.

Data on these indicators were sourced from ASEANStats, the ADB Key Indicators Database, and other publicly available databases of international organizations. As of this writing, much of the available data is only for 2000 to 2019. Thus, this report does not cover the extent of change in development progress and trajectory in ASEAN due to the COVID-19 pandemic. However, two boxes on learning poverty and expected learning losses from pandemic-induced school closures, and on coverage of social protection in ASEAN member states as of 2020 are provided.

Further, the report includes a convergence analysis to measure progress in narrowing development gaps for a selection of indicators. Two types of convergence have been discussed: (i) Beta-convergence, which examines whether less-developed ASEAN member states have grown faster than more developed ones; and (ii) Sigma-convergence, which examines whether the gaps among ASEAN member states have reduced over time. Previous studies have applied Beta- and/or Sigma-convergence analysis to indicators, including the Human Development Index (HDI) and its components, and other health and education outcomes (Hrzic et al. 2020, Bunnag 2019, Janssen et al. 2016, Jorda and Sarabia 2015, Bucur and O.A. Stangaciu 2015). At the minimum, we conduct convergence analysis for GDP per capita, which was featured in the first AFEED Monitor (World Bank 2014, Figure 11, p. 9).

Development indicators tracked in this report broadly describe socioeconomic conditions across ASEAN member states. They provide a broad picture of the progress of the ASEAN community in achieving a range of development outcomes and policies, which are either intrinsic to narrowing the development gap or the pursuit of equitable and sustainable development. These include the eradication of poverty, reduction of maternal and child deaths, universal access to basic education, eradication of malnutrition, gender equality and social inclusion, digital access and skills, climate and disaster resilience—or instrumental to these development goals— such as economic growth, macroeconomic stability, decent work, greater access to finance, good governance, environmental protection, and sound regulatory policies. Measurements in the indicator system of this report can be used as inputs by individual ASEAN member states for identifying priority areas for policy action, and for collective interventions across the ASEAN community.

# II.   OVERALL HUMAN DEVELOPMENT

Although GDP is a well-known yardstick of economic performance, policy choices can be inadequate if there is overreliance on this measure as it does not inform everything about the conditions of countries and societies (Stiglitz, Fitoussi, and Durand 2018). This is why dashboards of indicators, such as the Global Indicators for Measuring the Sustainable Development Indicators, or composite indicators, such as the HDI, the Social Progress Index,[7] and Multidimensional Poverty Index[8] have been developed and used.

In its human development reports that have been released since 1990, the United Nations Development Programme (UNDP) discusses the HDI, a summary measure of average achievements in key human development dimensions, i.e., health, education, and standard of living (UNDP 1990). All these metrics, aside from data dashboards on indicator frameworks, including the global indicators for monitoring the SDGs, reveal patterns of growth and development, and with disaggregated data, we can determine who benefits from growth, and what factors contribute to a country's progress.

In 2000–2019, the region's HDI increased by 0.9% per year, on average, from 0.61 in 2000 to 0.73 in 2019. The gap in the human development between ASEAN-6 and CLMV has noticeably narrowed in the same period, albeit quite slowly across the years since 2000 (Table 2).

**Table 2: Human Development Index in ASEAN-6 and Cambodia, the Lao People's Democratic Republic, Myanmar, and Viet Nam, 2000–2019**

| Economies | 2000–2004 | 2005–2009 | 2010–2014 | 2015–2019 |
|-----------|-----------|-----------|-----------|-----------|
| ASEAN-6   | 0.67      | 0.70      | 0.73      | 0.75      |
| CLMV      | 0.57      | 0.61      | 0.65      | 0.67      |
| ASEAN     | 0.63      | 0.66      | 0.70      | 0.72      |

ASEAN = Association of Southeast Asian Nations; ASEAN-6 = Association of Southeast Asian Nations comprising Brunei Darussalam, Indonesia, Malaysia, the Philippines, Singapore, and Thailand.
Source: United Nations Development Programme. Human Development Index. https://hdr.undp.org/data-center/human-development-index#/indicies/HDI (accessed 21 August 2022).

---

[7]   The Social Progress Imperative regularly releases the Social Progress Index, which, like the HDI, is based on social outcomes, but unlike HDI, it includes other indicators such as institutional, environmental, equity, and inclusion factors.

[8]   Two recent benchmarks on multidimensional poverty measurement are the Global Multidimensional Poverty Index of UNDP/OPHI (UNDP 2010, Alkire and Foster 2011, Kovacevic and Calderon 2014, Alkire et al. 2018) and the Multidimensional Poverty Measures of World Bank (World Bank 2018). Both measurement systems enable a comparison of multidimensional poverty conditions across countries and over time. Several ASEAN member states, together with other developing countries, have been motivated to develop their own national measures of multidimensional poverty, alongside monetary poverty measures, as headline summaries of poverty and welfare conditions.

# III. MATERIAL WELL-BEING

Despite the limitations of GDP, it is still, however, the most well-known measure of economic performance. From 2000 to 2019, economic growth in ASEAN has, on average, grown by 5.2% per year, with growth even stronger in CLMV (7.1%) than in ASEAN-6 (4.9%). The region's economic performance slowed down given the mobility restrictions during the onset of the pandemic, leading to a contraction of the GDP in ASEAN-6 by 4.7%, and a reduced 2020 growth in GDP in CLMV to 2.6% (which declined from 7% in the previous year).

Upward income convergence was also being achieved before 2020, with the ratio of GDP per capita of ASEAN-6 to CLMV decreasing from 3.4 in 2000 to 2.1 in 2019 (Figure 4). However, the COVID-19 pandemic—unlike the 2008 global financial crisis that slightly accelerated income convergence in the region a year later—has further accelerated income convergence with the ratio of GDP of ASEAN-6 to CLMV reaching its lowest point of 2.0. In 2021, the trajectory had a slight divergence as economic recovery accelerated in ASEAN-6 (especially in Singapore) much more than in CLMV.

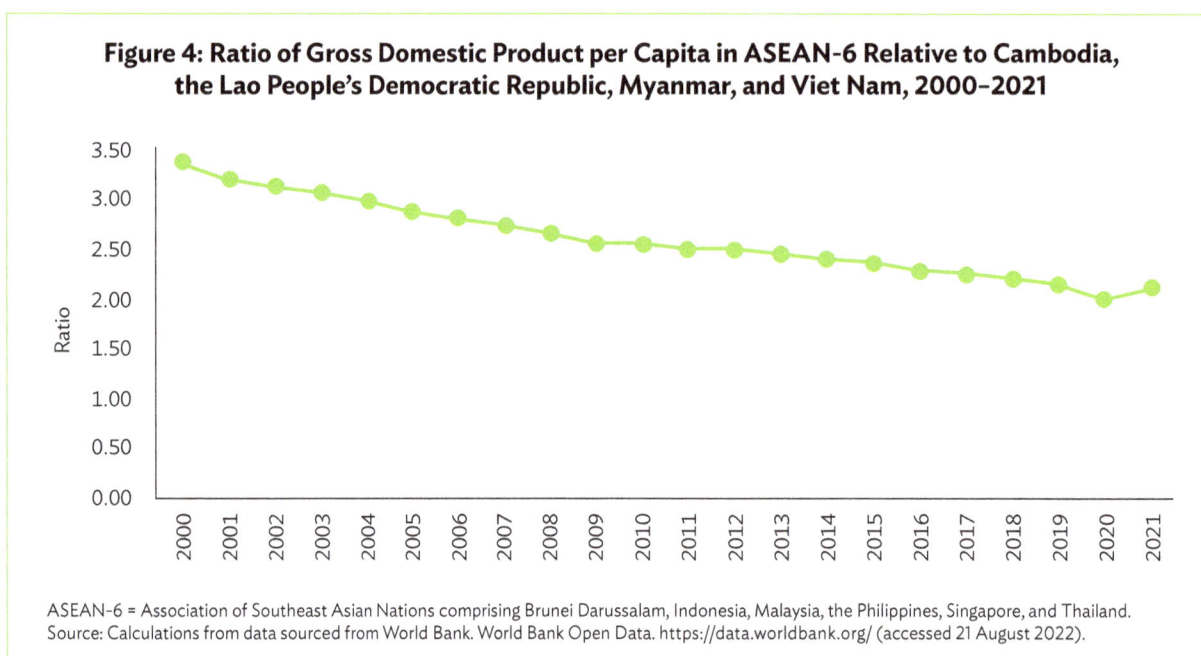

**Figure 4: Ratio of Gross Domestic Product per Capita in ASEAN-6 Relative to Cambodia, the Lao People's Democratic Republic, Myanmar, and Viet Nam, 2000–2021**

ASEAN-6 = Association of Southeast Asian Nations comprising Brunei Darussalam, Indonesia, Malaysia, the Philippines, Singapore, and Thailand.
Source: Calculations from data sourced from World Bank. World Bank Open Data. https://data.worldbank.org/ (accessed 21 August 2022).

The region's rapid economic growth in the last 2 decades contributed to the significant reductions in the proportion of people living in absolute poverty (Figure 5). The proportion of ASEAN people living in extreme poverty, i.e., below the international poverty line[9] of $2.15 per person per day in purchasing power parity (PPP) 2017 prices, fell to less than one-in-30 persons (3.3%) in 2019 from about one-in-three persons (36.6%) in 2000.

---

[9]　Presently, the international poverty line used for monitoring extreme poverty is $2.15 in PPP 2011 prices. A PPP "between two countries, A and B, is the ratio of the number of units of country A's currency needed to purchase in country A the same quantity of a specific good or service as one unit of country B's currency will purchase in country B. PPPs can be expressed in the currency of either of the countries. In practice, they are usually computed among large numbers of countries and expressed in terms of a single currency, with the US dollar most commonly used as the base or 'numeraire currency' (World Bank 2008).

In CLMV, extreme poverty declined by 47.1 percentage points from about half (48.4% in 2000 to nearly one-in-100 persons [1.2%] in 2019) shortly before the onset of the COVID-19 pandemic. Meanwhile in ASEAN-6, the proportion of people with incomes below $2.15 reduced by 25.0 percentage points in the same period to 3.4% in 2019. Although a poverty line of $2.15 per person per day in 2017 PPP prices is relevant for measuring poverty in low-income countries, higher lines are more relevant for measuring poverty in higher-income countries. All ASEAN member states are either lower-middle-income or upper-middle-income countries. The World Bank suggests that poverty lines of $3.65 (in PPP 2017 prices) and $6.85 (in PPP 2017 prices) are more applicable for monitoring poverty in lower-middle-income and upper-middle-income countries, respectively. When examining poverty in ASEAN-6 and CLMV with higher international poverty lines, such as $3.65 per day, the reductions are noticeably less sharp. Further, regardless of the poverty line used, the rates of reduction in poverty have been less in recent years.

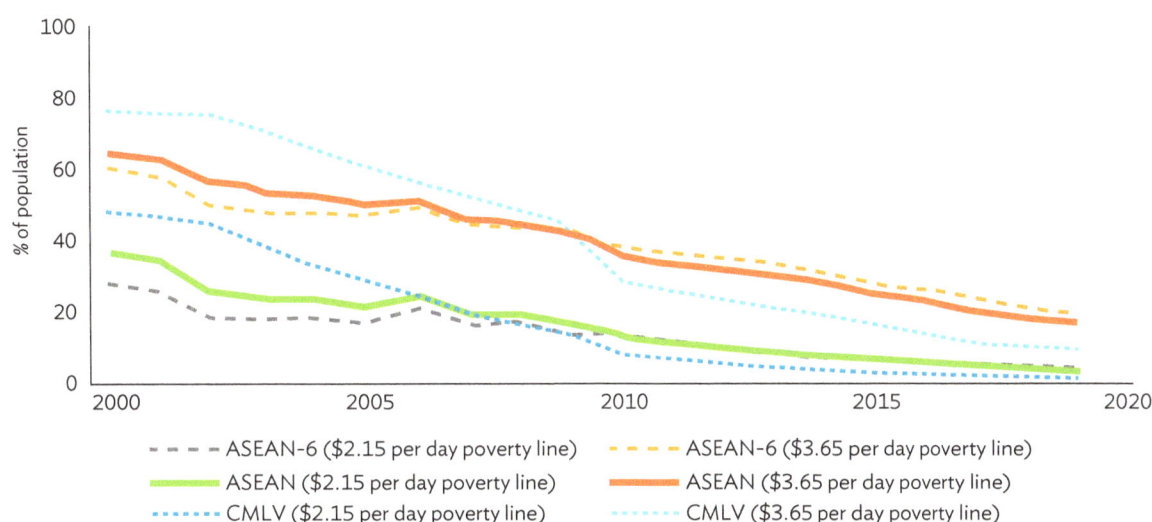

**Figure 5: Poverty in ASEAN-6 and Cambodia, the Lao People's Democratic Republic, Myanmar, and Viet Nam, 2000–2019**

ASEAN = Association of Southeast Asian Nations; ASEAN-6 = Association of Southeast Asian Nations comprising Brunei Darussalam, Indonesia, Malaysia, the Philippines, Singapore, and Thailand; CLMV = Cambodia, the Lao People's Democratic Republic, Myanmar, and Viet Nam.
Source: World Bank. 2022. Poverty and Inequality Platform. World Bank Group. https://pip.worldbank.org/home (accessed 8 January 2023).

Poverty is commonly comprehended as a lack of well-being. It has been typically measured in terms of deprivation in a monetary indicator of welfare, either income- or consumption-based (although countries have also begun to measure multidimensional poverty). The percentage of the population in extreme poverty having incomes or consumptions below the international poverty line of $2.15 PPP per person per day (in 2017 PPP prices) is a simple, comparable measure of extreme poverty across ASEAN member states. It helps assess overall progress in reducing extreme poverty. Extreme poverty has been at 5% or less for most ASEAN member states before the pandemic.

Table 3 shows that according to recent data, the proportion of the population below $2.15 is near zero in Malaysia and Thailand, below 5% in Viet Nam (1.2%), Myanmar (2.0%), the Philippines (3.0%), and Indonesia (3.5%), and at 7.1% in the Lao PDR. Further, poverty has decreased in 2000 to 2021 because of high economic growth.[10]

---

[10]    ASEAN member states that measure poverty make use of their own national poverty lines to monitor changes in poverty, as well as evaluate policies, programs, and strategies for reducing poverty. Across member states, while methodologies for determining national poverty lines are typically based on determination of the cost of basic food and non-food needs for a minimum welfare standard, the approaches vary reflecting national priorities and standards. Thus, cross-country comparisons using national poverty lines (and poverty rates) are challenging given differences in methodologies for setting the poverty line, differences in choices of welfare indicators, and differences in survey questionnaires for collecting the welfare indicator across countries.

While poverty may have increased because of lockdowns to reduce infections during the onset of the pandemic, it is likely that ASEAN member states will still reach zero poverty by 2030 given the economic recovery experienced in the region. The recovery may also be fragile given the effects of the Russian invasion of Ukraine (ASEAN 2022b).

**Table 3: Gross Domestic Product Growth and Extreme Poverty in ASEAN Member States, 2000–2021**

| ASEAN Member State | Annual GDP Growth (2000–2021) | Proportion of Population in Extreme Poverty below the International Poverty Line ($2.15 per person per day in 2017 purchasing power parity prices) | |
|---|---|---|---|
| | | Earliest Year | Latest Year |
| Indonesia | 4.84 | 43.6  (2000) | 3.5  (2021) |
| Lao PDR | 6.60 | 25.4  (2002) | 7.1  (2018) |
| Malaysia | 4.24 | 1.6  (2003) | 0.0  (2018) |
| Myanmar | 7.85 | 6.2  (2015) | 2.0  (2017) |
| Philippines | 4.76 | 14.5  (2000) | 3.0  (2018) |
| Thailand | 3.31 | 4.0  (2000) | 0.0  (2020) |
| Viet Nam | 6.20 | 29.9  (2002) | 1.2  (2018) |

ASEAN = Association of Southeast Asian Nations, GDP = gross domestic product, Lao PDR = Lao People's Democratic Republic.
Source: World Bank. World Bank Open Data. https://data.worldbank.org/ (accessed 8 January 2023).

The international poverty line of $2.15 is not relevant in middle-income countries. Using a poverty line of $3.65 (in PPP 2017 prices), the proportion in poverty across lower-middle-income member states currently ranges from 5.3% (in Viet Nam) to 32.5% (in the Lao PDR); while using a poverty line of $6.85 (in PPP 2017 prices), poverty in upper-middle income ASEAN member states is estimated in recent years at 4.8% in Malaysia and at 13.2% in Thailand (Table 4).

**Table 4: Proportion of People in Poverty in ASEAN Member States, 2000–2021**
(using lower- and upper-middle-income international poverty lines)

| ASEAN Member State | Proportion of Population below the International Poverty Line for Lower-Middle-Income Countries ($3.65 per day in 2017 purchasing power parity prices) | | Proportion of Population below the International Poverty Line for Upper-Middle-Income Countries ($6.85 per day in 2017 purchasing power parity prices) | |
|---|---|---|---|---|
| | Earliest Year | Latest Year | Earliest Year | Latest Year |
| Indonesia | 81.6  (2000) | 22.4  (2021) | 96.9  (2000) | 60.6  (2021) |
| Lao PDR* | 65.3  (2002) | 32.5  (2018) | 91.9  (2002) | 70.5  (2018) |
| Malaysia** | 8.2  (2003) | 0.4  (2018) | 27.8  (2003) | 4.8  (2018) |
| Myanmar* | 30.0  (2015) | 19.6  (2017) | 72.8  (2015) | 68.2  (2017) |
| Philippines* | 39.2  (2000) | 18.3  (2018) | 68.8  (2000) | 53.4  (2018) |
| Thailand** | 23.5  (2000) | 0.7  (2020) | 59.0  (2000) | 13.2  (2020) |
| Viet Nam* | 65.6  (2002) | 5.3  (2018) | 88.9  (2002) | 22.2  (2018) |

ASEAN = Association of Southeast Asian Nations, Lao PDR = Lao People's Democratic Republic.
Note: * lower middle income; ** upper middle income
Source: World Bank. World Bank Open Data. https://data.worldbank.org/ (accessed 8 January 2023).

# IV. EMPLOYMENT AND WORKING CONDITIONS

ASEAN has sought to promote decent work in the region, but progress has been challenging in the jobs agenda across ASEAN member states. Even before the pandemic, the Lao PDR's unemployment rate was at 9.4%, while most member states had unemployment rates in 2015–2019 within about 1 percentage point from their corresponding rates in 2000–2004. The exceptions are Indonesia and Cambodia, which have been successful in reducing unemployment in 2015–2019 by around 2 percentage points, from rates in 2000–2004. Progress in narrowing the gap in employment between ASEAN-6 and CLMV is difficult to assess given substantially varying employment conditions across member states, i.e., a considerable portion of the employed population in CLMV works in the informal sector and in vulnerable employment even outside of the agriculture sector (Table 5 and ASEAN 2019).

The pandemic further worsened unemployment, with rates increasing in all ASEAN member states where data is available (Figure 6).

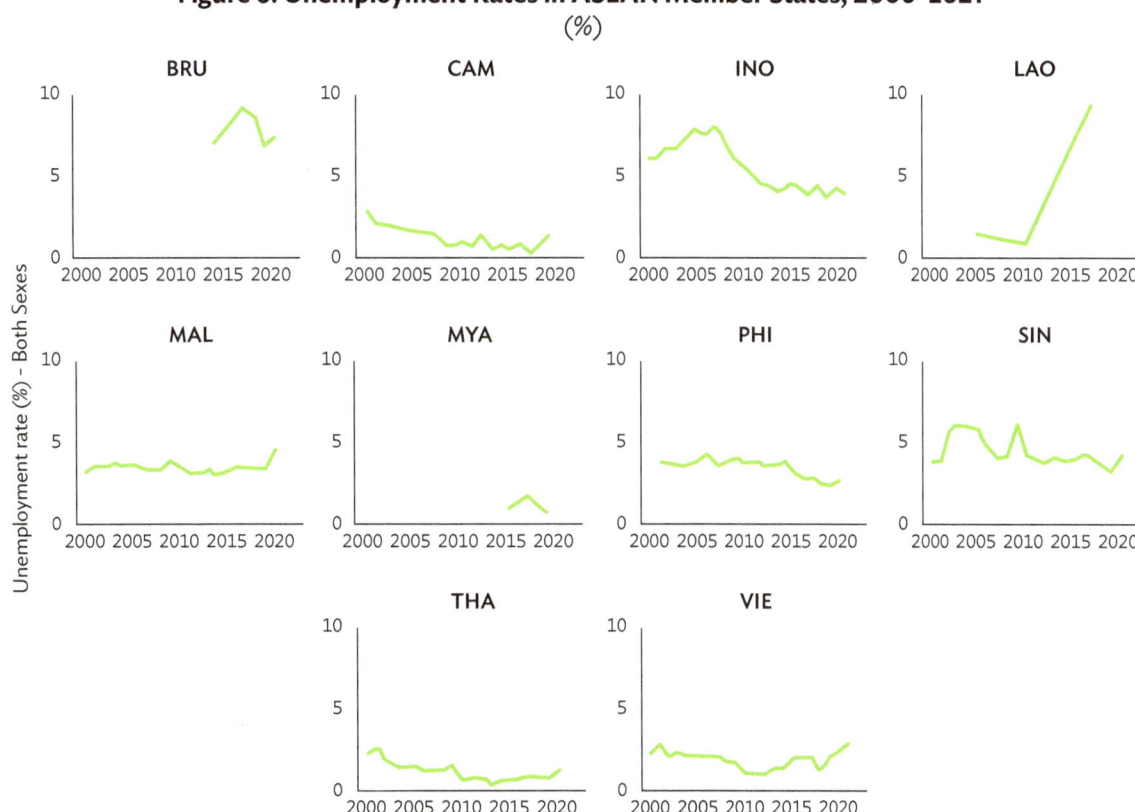

**Figure 6: Unemployment Rates in ASEAN Member States, 2000–2021**
(%)

ASEAN = Association of Southeast Asian Nations, BRU = Brunei Darussalam, CAM = Cambodia, INO = Indonesia, LAO = Lao People's Democratic Republic, MAL = Malaysia, MYA = Myanmar, PHI = Philippines, SIN = Singapore, THA = Thailand, VIE = Viet Nam.
Source: United Nations Department of Economic and Social Affairs. 2021. Sustainable Development Goals (SDG) Global Database. https://unstats.un.org/sdgs/dataportal (accessed 21 August 2022).

The COVID-19 pandemic affected people differently. The impact of the pandemic on males and females varied across ASEAN member states (Figure 7). The rise of unemployment in member states is noticeably higher among females than males in Brunei Darussalam, Malaysia, and Viet Nam; lower for females in Indonesia and the Philippines; and the same for both sexes in Singapore and Thailand. According to UN Women (2015), women's economic empowerment has been greatly reduced during the onset of the pandemic in several ASEAN member states. Further, women have been bearing the brunt of increased unpaid care work responsibilities.

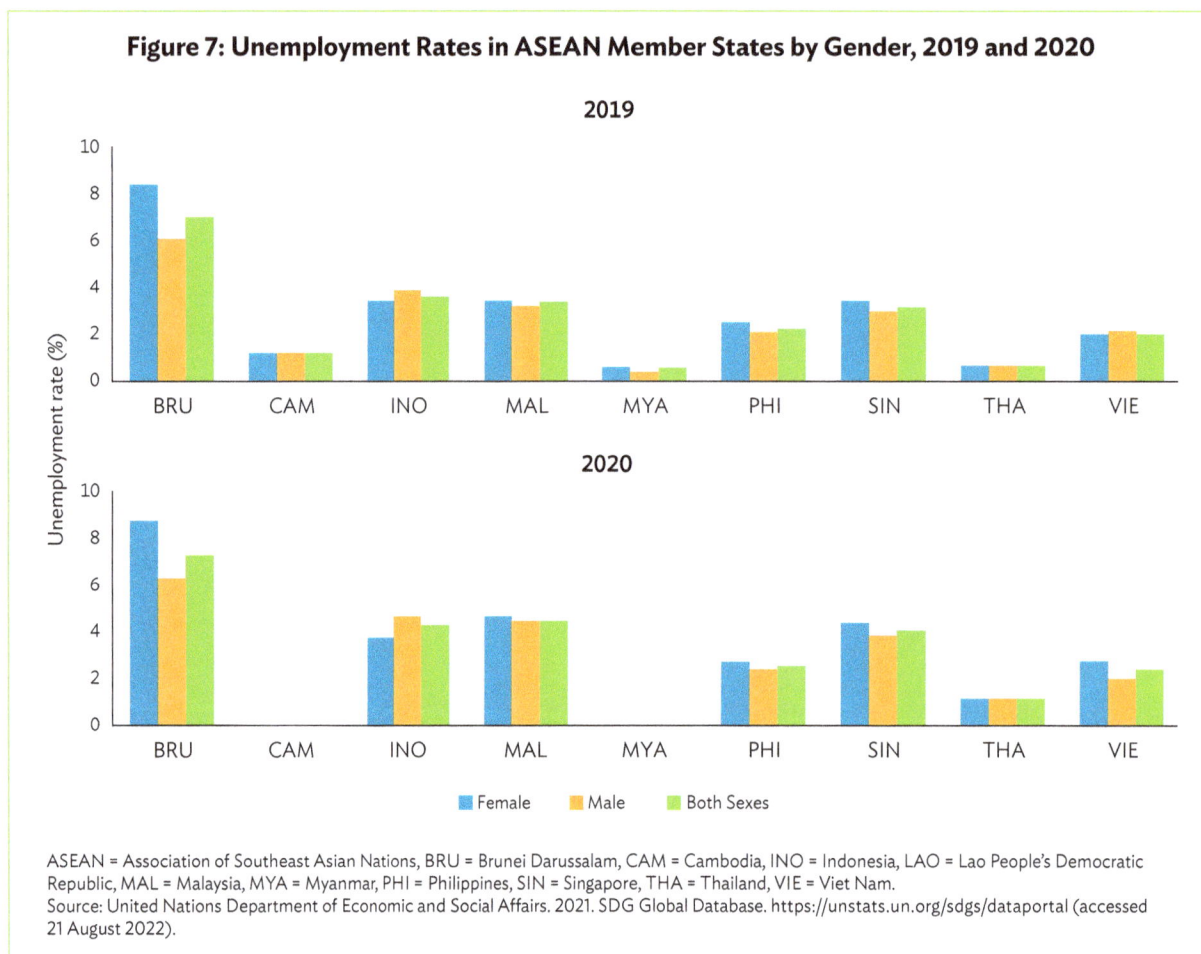

**Figure 7: Unemployment Rates in ASEAN Member States by Gender, 2019 and 2020**

ASEAN = Association of Southeast Asian Nations, BRU = Brunei Darussalam, CAM = Cambodia, INO = Indonesia, LAO = Lao People's Democratic Republic, MAL = Malaysia, MYA = Myanmar, PHI = Philippines, SIN = Singapore, THA = Thailand, VIE = Viet Nam.
Source: United Nations Department of Economic and Social Affairs. 2021. SDG Global Database. https://unstats.un.org/sdgs/dataportal (accessed 21 August 2022).

Although unemployment is a popular indicator of the labor market, cross-country comparisons need to be done with caution given that a considerable portion of employed population in some ASEAN member states work in the informal sector and in vulnerable employment. Those in informal and vulnerable employment are without access to benefits of formal, non-vulnerable employment such as sick pay, leave, and pensions. In most ASEAN member states for which data are available, the proportion of men and women who are informally employed is similar, but within this kind of work, there are gender issues. In several ASEAN member states, the bulk of informal employment of men is concentrated in informal enterprises where they are employers or employees, which, while providing insecure employment, still attracts better pay. On the other hand, women tend to be own-account workers and contributing family workers—two categories of informal work where people employed are poorly paid, face a high level of job insecurity, and have no access to social protection especially for periods of low economic demand for products and services, or when they cannot work or cannot find work. Further, even as women work in informal employment, they are more likely than men to work from their own homes, where their invisibility increases their vulnerability.

Informal employment in nonagricultural employment is less than half in Brunei Darussalam, and about half in Thailand and Viet Nam (Table 5). Meanwhile, in Cambodia, Indonesia, the Lao PDR, Malaysia, and Myanmar, more than half of those engaged in informal employment work outside of agriculture. Brunei Darussalam, Cambodia, and Viet Nam have a bigger share of males than females with jobs in the informal nonagricultural sector, while the reverse is the case for Indonesia, the Lao PDR, Myanmar, and Thailand. Since the pandemic, a slight increase in the share of males engaged in informal employment outside of the agriculture sector was recorded in Brunei Darussalam and in Viet Nam.

**Table 5: Proportion of Informal Employment in Nonagricultural Employment by Gender, 2019–2021**

| ASEAN Member State | 2019 | | | 2020–2021 | | |
|---|---|---|---|---|---|---|
| | Female | Male | Both Sexes | Female | Male | Both Sexes |
| Brunei Darussalam | 28.9 | 31.9 | 30.7 | 25.4** | 32.7** | 29.8** |
| Cambodia | 82.0 | 84.3 | 83.2 | | | |
| Indonesia | 76.0 | 73.9 | 74.7 | | | |
| Lao PDR | 79.5* | 71.5* | 75.2* | | | |
| Myanmar | 81.3 | 78.0 | 79.6 | | | |
| Thailand | 53.0* | 51.0* | 51.9* | | | |
| Viet Nam | 49.2 | 58.5 | 54.2 | 49.6 | 59.6 | 54.9 |

ASEAN = Association of Southeast Asian Nations, Lao PDR = Lao People's Democratic Republic.
Note: * 2018; ** 2020 only.
Source: United Nations Department of Economic and Social Affairs. 2021. SDG Global Database. https://unstats.un.org/sdgs/dataportal (accessed 22 August 2022).

Across ASEAN member states, youths aged 15–24 have a much larger unemployment rate than adults aged 25 and over. Further, among the youth who are neither employed, studying, or in training (not in employment, education, or training [NEET]), only Brunei Darussalam and Singapore are successful in having less than 10% youth NEET rates. In ASEAN-6, the average youth NEET rate is lower (15%) by 4.4 percentage points from that of CLMV (19.4%). The youth NEET data is important as being NEET can undermine the youth's future employment and earning prospects and can lead to adverse social consequences.

# V.    ACCESS TO FINANCE

The ASEAN community has sought to improve financial inclusion, i.e., the use of financial services by individuals and firms. Access to finance allows people to save for retirement and establish businesses to increase opportunities. The benefits produced by financial intermediation and markets should be spread widely enough throughout the population and across firms and economic sectors. Assets of the financial system should not be concentrated in relatively few persons, firms, or sectors. Measures of financial inclusion consist of density indicators, such as the number of bank branches or ATMs per capita, and "user-side" indicators, such as account ownership. A bank account can help poor people save for the future. Lack of a bank account or a mobile money account can be quite costly to low-income families as they conduct financial transactions at alternative providers. In addition, poor people need mechanisms to foster savings for the future.

Obtaining an account with a mobile money provider has been increasing in ASEAN. Since 2012, the number of registered mobile money accounts per 1,000 adults has been increasing in ASEAN member states, though at different rates and from various starting points (Figure 8). Mobile money accounts have even nearly doubled for some members states, and more than doubled for others during the pandemic.

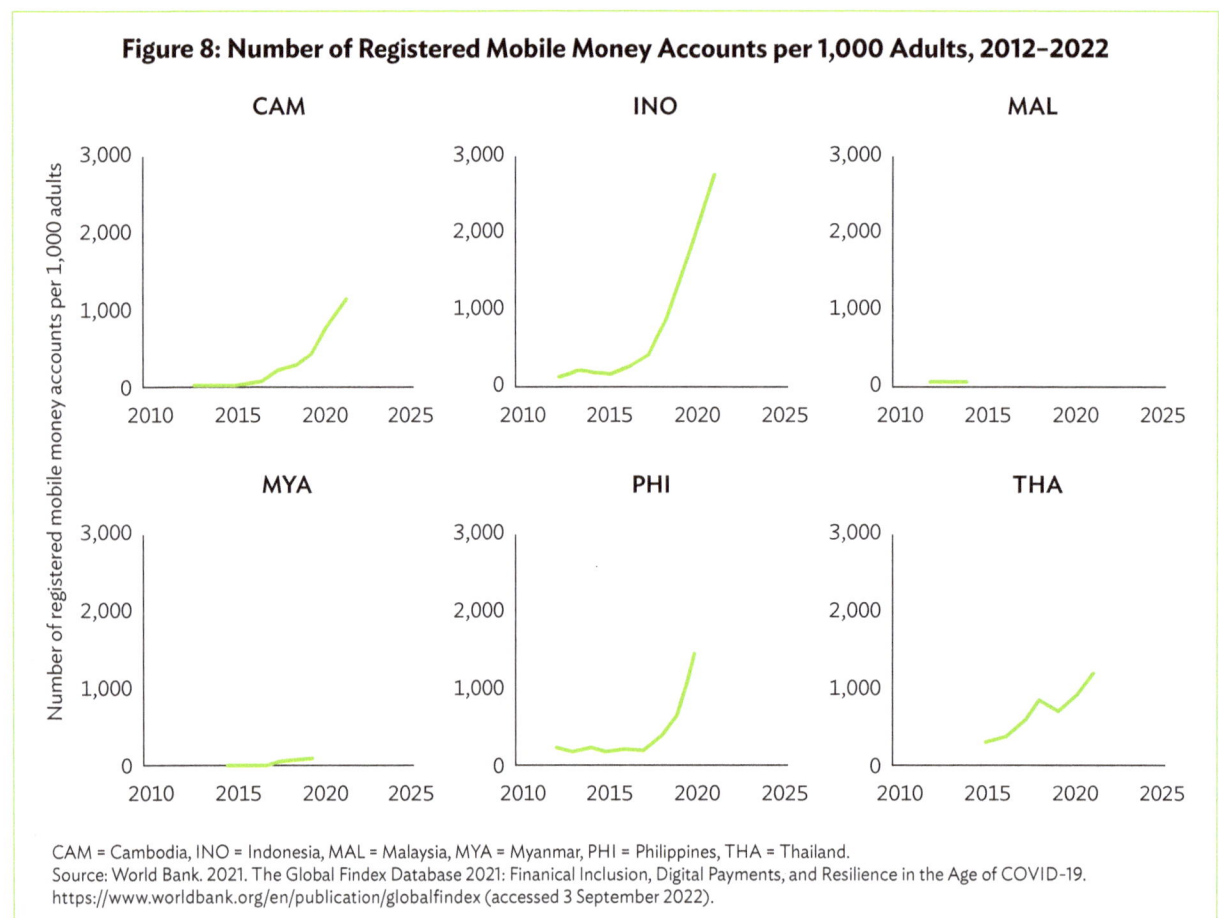

Figure 8: Number of Registered Mobile Money Accounts per 1,000 Adults, 2012–2022

CAM = Cambodia, INO = Indonesia, MAL = Malaysia, MYA = Myanmar, PHI = Philippines, THA = Thailand.
Source: World Bank. 2021. The Global Findex Database 2021: Finanical Inclusion, Digital Payments, and Resilience in the Age of COVID-19. https://www.worldbank.org/en/publication/globalfindex (accessed 3 September 2022).

In consequence, the proportion of the population within ASEAN member states that own a bank account or an account with a mobile money service provider has improved amid the pandemic, compared to baselines in 2017 (Figure 9). Across CLMV, a quarter (26.9%), on average, of their populations aged 15 and over held an account at a financial institution or with a mobile money service provider as of 2017. On the other hand, in 2017, seven out of 10 (69.6%) persons aged 15 and above, on average, in ASEAN-6 owned accounts at a financial institution or with a mobile money service provider. The corresponding proportions, though varied from about a third (34.5%) in the Philippines to nearly everyone (97.9%) in Singapore. Data in 2021 suggest all ASEAN member states increased ownership of accounts at a financial institution or with a mobile money service provider, though the proportions remain below half of the population aged 15 and over in Cambodia (33.3%), the Lao PDR (37.3%), and Myanmar (47.8%).

**Figure 9: Proportion of Population Aged 15 and Over Owning an Account at a Financial Institution or Mobile Money Service Provider, 2017 and 2021** (%)

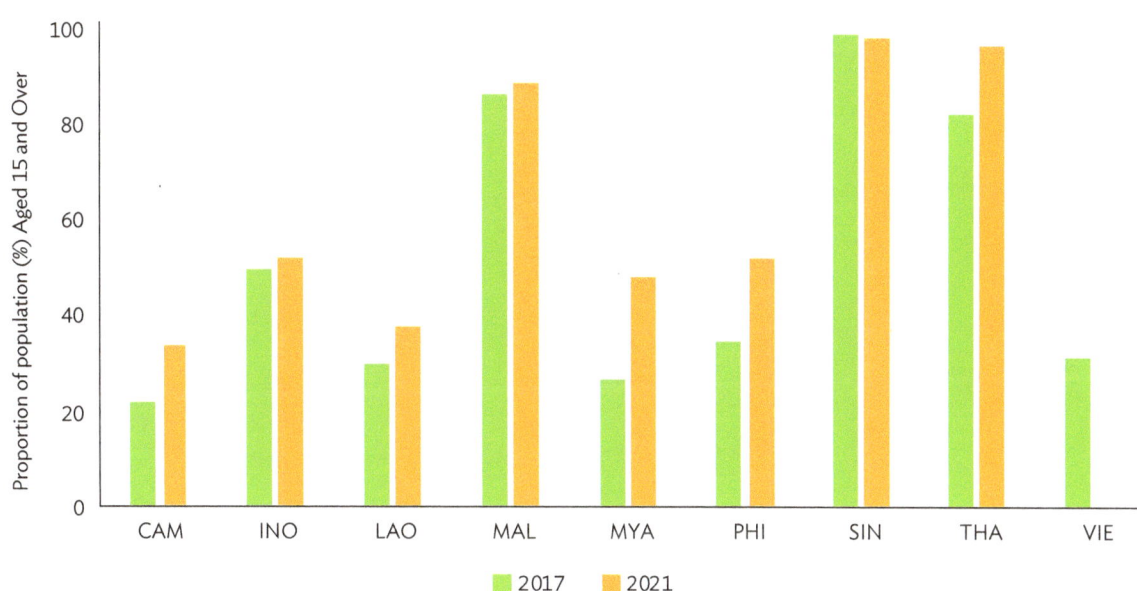

BRU = Brunei Darussalam, CAM = Cambodia, INO = Indonesia, LAO = Lao People's Democratic Republic, MAL = Malaysia, MYA = Myanmar, PHI = Philippines, SIN = Singapore, THA = Thailand, VIE = Viet Nam.
Source: World Bank. 2021. The Global Findex Database 2021: Finanical Inclusion, Digital Payments, and Resilience in the Age of COVID-19. https://www.worldbank.org/en/publication/globalfindex (accessed 3 September 2022).

Table 6 provides data prior to and during the pandemic on density indicators. In five ASEAN member states—Brunei Darussalam, Cambodia, the Lao PDR, the Philippines, and Viet Nam—the number of ATMs per 100,000 adults increased from their levels in 2019, to those in 2020 to 2021. The number of commercial bank branches (per 100,000 adults), however, declined since 2019 in many member states where data is available, except for Cambodia and Viet Nam.

**Table 6: Selected Indicators on Access to Finance, 2019–2021**

| ASEAN Member State | Commercial Bank Branches (per 100,000 adults) | | Number of ATMs per 100,000 Adults | |
| --- | --- | --- | --- | --- |
| | 2019 | 2020–2021* | 2019 | 2020–2021* |
| Brunei Darussalam | 17.6 | 16.8 | 74.0 | 74.1 |
| Cambodia | 8.3 | 12.0 | 23.3 | 29.0 |
| Indonesia | 15.6 | 15.5 | 53.4 | 49.9 |
| Lao PDR | 3.2 | 3.2 | 26.9 | 27.7 |
| Malaysia | 10.1 | 8.8 | 56.1 | 54.9 |
| Myanmar | 5.6 | | 6.9 | |
| Philippines | 9.2 | 9.1 | 29.0 | 29.6 |
| Singapore | 7.8 | 7.0 | 58.8 | 54.2 |
| Thailand | 11.2 | 10.1 | 115.1 | 110.0 |
| Viet Nam | 4.0 | 3.5 | 25.9 | 26.7 |

ASEAN = Association of Southeast Asian Nations, ATM = automated teller machine, Lao PDR = Lao People's Democratic Republic.
Note: * averaged for the period.
Source: International Monetary Fund. Financial Access Survey. https://data.imf.org/fas (accessed 3 September 2022).

# VI.   HEALTH AND NUTRITION

All people in the ASEAN community have a right to live, eat, and stay healthy. Providing adequate health-care services within and across the ASEAN community is a challenge, given interconnections of access to health care for everyone with poverty, water and sanitation, as well as with peace, stability, and governance. While ASEAN has attained significant progress over the years in meeting food security and nutritional needs within the region, hunger and malnutrition persist. Children are especially vulnerable to food insecurity and malnutrition. Attaining ASEAN Vision 2025 is extremely challenging as the pandemic has shown weaknesses in the public health systems of many member states. ASEAN should build resilient health-care systems; improve reproductive, maternal, and child health; reduce the impact of both communicable and noncommunicable diseases; achieve universal health coverage; and ensure access to safe, affordable, and effective medicines and vaccines for all, especially among those with a high risk of disease and death. Further, the region needs to have in place interventions for eradicating hunger, malnutrition, and food insecurity.

In ASEAN, the number of women dying during pregnancy, childbirth, and soon after, has fallen in member states, on average, by about half of maternal deaths from 199 deaths per 100,000 live births in 2000, to 104 in 2017 (Figure 10). While CLMV had much more maternal deaths (360 deaths) compared to ASEAN-6 (92 deaths) in 2000, it also had a bigger drop of 55.7% in maternal deaths. A decline of 25 fewer deaths resulted in ASEAN-6 from 2000 to 2017, but ASEAN-6 already had fewer (92) maternal deaths compared to CLMV as of 2000. From 2000 to 2017, maternal deaths have decreased in nearly all member states. The only exception is Brunei Darussalam, where maternal deaths have been low, ranging from 27 to 31 deaths per 100,000 live births in the same period.

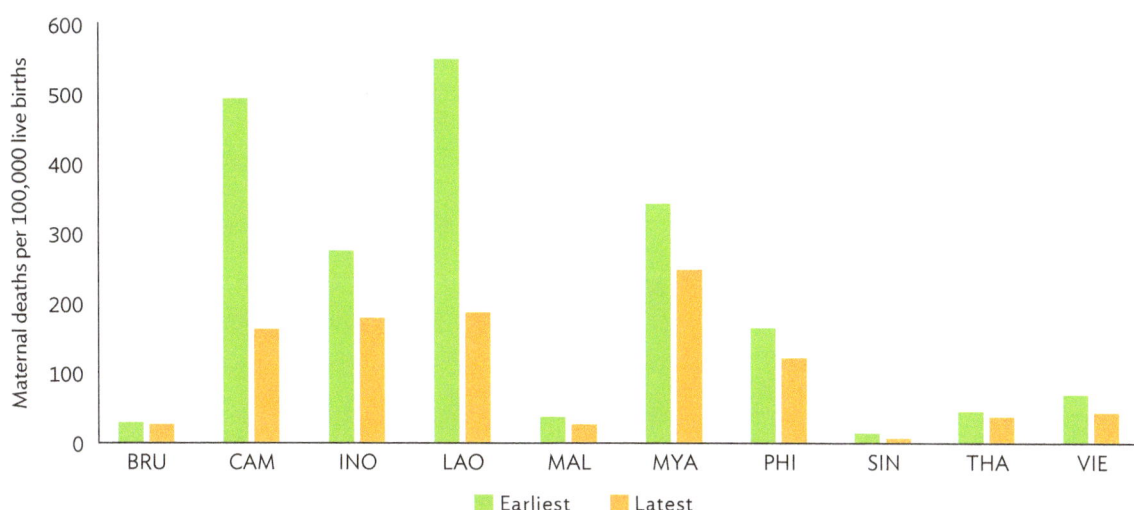

Figure 10: Maternal Mortality Rate: Earliest and Latest Years, 2000–2017

BRU = Brunei Darussalam, CAM = Cambodia, INO = Indonesia, LAO = Lao People's Democratic Republic, MAL = Malaysia, MYA = Myanmar, PHI = Philippines, SIN = Singapore, THA = Thailand, VIE = Viet Nam.
Source: United Nations Department of Economic and Social Affairs. 2021. SDG Global Database. https://unstats.un.org/sdgs/dataportal (accessed 10 August 2022).

Maternal deaths have gone down considerably from about 200 deaths per 100,000 live births in 2000–2004, to about half, i.e., 107 deaths in 2015–2019. Alongside the reduction in maternal mortality, member states have improved the access of expectant mothers to skilled birth attendants (Figure 11).

### Figure 11: Maternal Mortality Rates and Proportion of Births Attended by Skilled Health Personnel in ASEAN Member States, 2000–2019 (%)

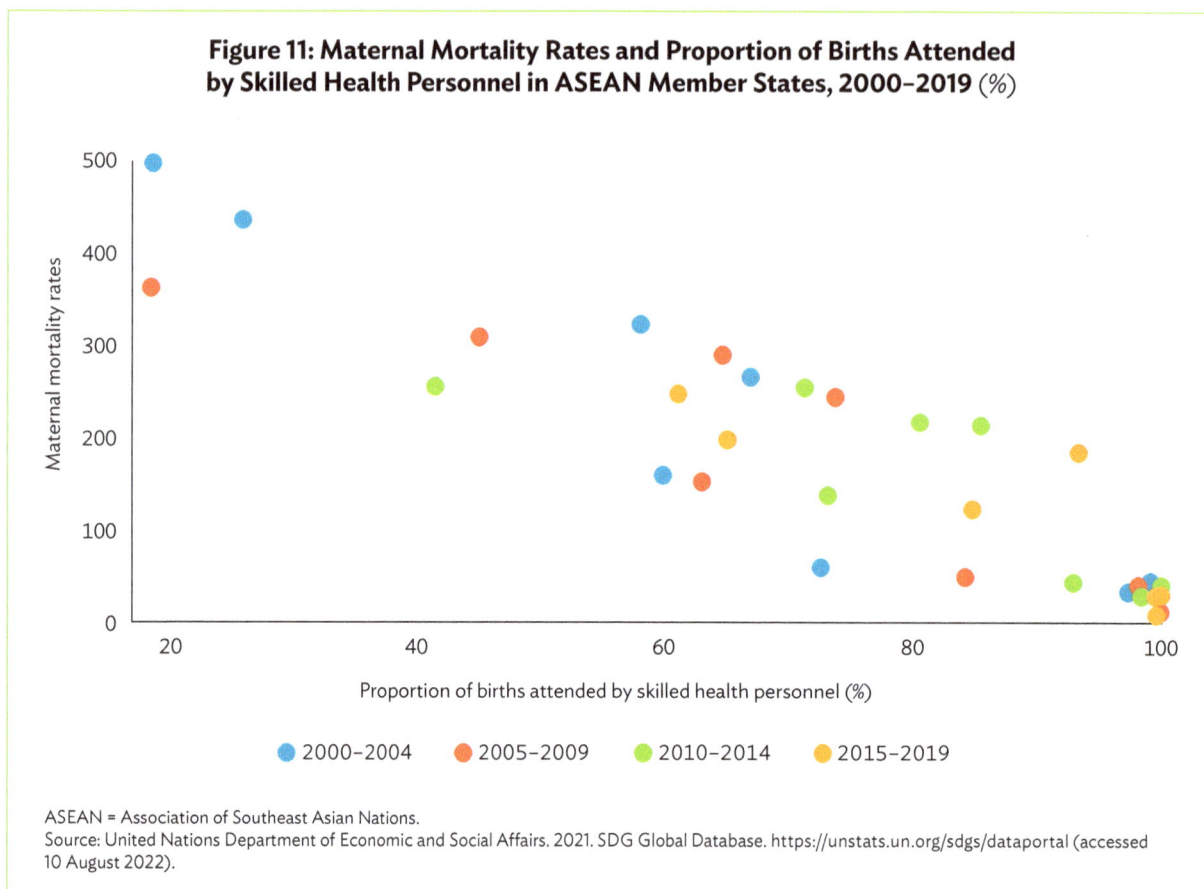

ASEAN = Association of Southeast Asian Nations.
Source: United Nations Department of Economic and Social Affairs. 2021. SDG Global Database. https://unstats.un.org/sdgs/dataportal (accessed 10 August 2022).

Whereas in 2000, only less than half (41.1%) of expectant mothers in CLMV received delivery care from a professional, by 2017, the proportion of expectant mothers receiving such care nearly doubled (77.4%). Nearly all CLMV had considerably improved their respective shares of births attended by skilled health personnel. Only Myanmar (3.2) had less than 5 percentage points improvement. Meanwhile, increases in the percentage of expectant mothers receiving delivery care ranged from 37.3 in Viet Nam to 57.2 percentage points in Cambodia. In ASEAN-6, the proportion of births attended by skilled health personnel improved by at most 5 percentage points or even declined in four countries from earliest to latest years in 2000 to 2017, but these member states already had more than 95% of expectant mothers receiving delivery care from skilled health personnel.

From 2000 to 2020, the number of children across ASEAN member states that die before age 5 had fallen on average by more than 54.2% (Table 7). The reduction has been sharper in CLMV at 59.6% reduction in the same period, compared to ASEAN-6's 41.0% drop in children under-5 who have died.

**Table 7: Selected Indicators on Children's Health and Nutrition, 2000–2020**

| ASEAN Member State | Under-5 Mortality Rates (per 1,000 liver births) | | Prevalence of Stunting, Height-for-Age (% of children under 5) | |
|---|---|---|---|---|
| | 2000 | 2020 | 2000 | 2020 |
| Brunei Darussalam | 10.3 | 11.5 | 20.9 | 12.7 |
| Cambodia | 106.3 | 25.7 | 49.0 | 29.9 |
| Indonesia | 52.2 | 23.0 | 42.4 | 31.8 |
| Lao PDR | 107.2 | 44.1 | 47.5 | 30.2 |
| Malaysia | 10.2 | 8.6 | 20.7 | 20.9 |
| Myanmar | 89.6 | 43.7 | 40.8 | 25.2 |
| Philippines | 37.7 | 26.4 | 35.7 | 28.7 |
| Singapore | 3.9 | 2.2 | 4.4 | 2.8 |
| Thailand | 22.0 | 8.7 | 16.9 | 12.3 |
| Viet Nam | 29.8 | 20.9 | 41.8 | 19.6 |

ASEAN = Association of Southeast Asian Nations, Lao PDR = Lao People's Democratic Republic.
Source: United Nations International Children's Emergency Fund (UNICEF), World Health Organization (WHO); World Bank. 2021. The UNICEF/WHO/WB Joint Child Malnutrition Estimates (JME) group released new data for 2021. https://www.who.int/data/gho/data/indicators/indicator-details/GHO/gho-jme-country-children-aged-5-years-stunted-(-height-for-age--2-sd) (accessed 3 September 2022).

Between 2000 and 2020, Cambodia had the highest average annual reduction in deaths of children under-5 by any ASEAN member state—from an under-5 mortality rate of 106 deaths per 1,000 live births in 2000 to about 26 deaths per 1,000 live births in 2020. The Lao PDR (63), Myanmar (46), and Indonesia (29) also had sizable drops in their respective under-5 mortality rates from 2000 to 2020. Reductions were more modest in Malaysia and Singapore, while child deaths even slightly increased in Brunei Darussalam, but these ASEAN member states have had a very low number of under-5 deaths (at around 10 or fewer deaths per 1,000 live births). As of 2020, the Lao PDR (44) and Myanmar (44) have the highest number of child deaths, followed by the Philippines (26), Cambodia (26), Indonesia (23), and Viet Nam (21).

The prevalence of stunting among children under-5 is a useful indicator of children's nutrition. When a child's height is below three standard deviations from the median weight-for-age, the child is said to be severely stunted, while if the weight is lower than two standard deviations from the growth standard but higher than three standard deviations, then the child is moderately stunted. In 2000, approximately a third (32%) of children in the region had stunted growths, i.e., had heights that fell below norms. This reduced to a fourth (24%) by 2020.

Like many development indicators examined thus far, the proportion of under-5 children with low-height-for-age suggests progress across the ASEAN community though achievements have been uneven. All CLMV have had more success (than ASEAN-6) in reducing in stunting prevalence rates for children under-5 years of age. Viet Nam led the reduction in the proportion of low-height-for-age under-5 children from 41.8% in 2000 to 19.6% in 2020. From 2000 to 2020, stunting prevalence among under-5 children also declined in Cambodia from 49.0% to 29.9%; in the Lao PDR from 47.5% to 30.2%; and in Myanmar from 40.8% to 25.2%. Expectedly, Singapore, which already had a very low level of stunting at 4.4% in 2000, observed a small reduction in stunting of 1.6 percentage points from 2000 to 2020. Malaysia even had a slight increase from 20.7% in 2000 to 20.9% in 2020. Gaps across ASEAN member states in the incidence of low height-for-age among children under-5 persist with the proportions ranging from 2.8% (in Singapore) to 31.8% (in Indonesia) as of 2020.

Data from select member states—Cambodia and Myanmar—suggest disparities in stunting across demographic groups (Table 8). Children from poor households, those residing in rural areas, and/or children with less-educated mothers are more likely to have stunted growths than their respective counterparts in rich households, urban areas, and families with mothers of higher educational attainment. Furthermore, in the case of Cambodia, gaps in stunting between the poorest and the richest households have persisted, while the urban–rural divide has even increased in the span of about 15 years.

**Table 8: Proportion of Children with Stunted Growth in Select ASEAN Member States by Residence, Education of Mother, and Wealth Quintile, 2000–2016** (%)

| ASEAN Member State | Year | Stunting Prevalence among Under-5 Children | | | | | | | | | |
|---|---|---|---|---|---|---|---|---|---|---|---|
| | | | Residence | | Education of Mother | | Wealth Quintile | | | | |
| | | Total | Urban | Rural | None or Primary | Secondary or Higher | Lowest | Second | Middle | Fourth | Highest |
| Cambodia | 2014 | 32.4 | 23.7 | 33.8 | 35.0 | 25.6 | 41.9 | 37.1 | 31.7 | 29.1 | 18.5 |
| Cambodia | 2010 | 39.9 | 27.5 | 42.2 | 41.8 | 30.7 | 51.1 | 44.4 | 39.3 | 34.2 | 23.1 |
| Cambodia | 2005 | 42.7 | 35.3 | 43.8 | 45.9 | 25.4 | 52.1 | 48.5 | 44.1 | 38.2 | 24.4 |
| Cambodia | 2000 | 49.8 | 42.4 | 51.0 | 52.1 | 39.1 | 58.0 | 53.0 | 47.9 | 48.6 | 32.8 |
| Myanmar | 2015–2016 | 29.2 | 20.0 | 31.6 | 33.3 | 21.1 | 38.0 | 31.9 | 29.1 | 21.1 | 16.0 |

ASEAN = Association of Southeast Asian Nations.
Source: ICF. 2012. The DHS Program STATcompiler. Funded by the United States Agency for International Development (USAID). http://www.statcompiler.com (accessed 21 August 2022).

# VII. EDUCATION

Since the adoption of the Universal Declaration of Human Rights in 1948, education has been recognized across countries as a human right.[11] Underlying the commitment to achieve various education goals and targets in the SDGs is recognition of the basic right, particularly of children, to quality education. Opportunities for learning, including quality education, relevant training, and opportunities for lifelong learning, should be accessible to everyone as learning plays a huge role in social inclusion.

Education strengthens capacities for functioning well in the labor market and society, thus ensuring equal access to economic opportunities and better income prospects, and consequently, leveraging opportunities for improved welfare. It increases prospects for learners to develop social skills. It exposes them to diverse experiences within a learning environment, thus enhancing social inclusion. The knowledge, skills and competencies gained by students from increased education offer possibilities to earn higher wages and find decent work. More education also enhances prospects for social mobility. Higher incomes enhance innovation and higher productivity, which, in turn, drive economic growth.

Education is a key driver for improving capabilities and opportunities for poor and vulnerable people and other marginalized sectors of society. Inclusive education not only empowers people but also leads to better health outcomes. Mothers with more educational attainment have larger chances of seeking pre- and post-natal care, assisted childbirth, and immunizations of their kids than those with less or no education. Children born to mothers who are literate are more likely to survive beyond 5 years of age. More educated mothers tend to have more educated children, with the accruing benefits slightly larger for girls than for boys (UNESCO 2014, ADB 2013). Young women who have completed primary education are found to be less likely to contract HIV than those with little or no schooling (Behrman 2015). Education inequalities translate into disparities in future skills—thus reducing education inequalities is imperative. Inclusive education facilitates equality of opportunity, social justice, and social inclusiveness, thereby improving chances for everyone, whether poor or nonpoor, disabled or not, males or females, urban or rural residents, to fully participate in development.

The ASEAN community collectively and individually have worked on developing basic human capabilities to enable everyone to participate in and benefit from growth processes. Table 9 lists data for select literacy indicators.[12] In 2016, functional literacy rates—the proportion of the population achieving at least a fixed level of proficiency in functional literacy skill—among those aged 15 years and above have been around 85% or better across ASEAN member states. These rates have improved in all but two member states in recent years with rates increasing by 0.1 percentage points (in Malaysia, Singapore, and Viet Nam) to 1.3 percentage points (in the Philippines). The exceptions are the Lao PDR and Cambodia where functional literacy decreased by 14.3 and 1.9 percentage points, respectively. Thus, gaps between ASEAN-6 and CLMV have widened in functional literacy. Simple literacy rates—i.e., the ability to read and write—have also improved in all ASEAN member states except for Myanmar.

---

[11]   This view has been affirmed in various global human rights treaties, such as the 1960 United Nations Educational, Scientific and Cultural Organization (UNESCO) Convention against Discrimination in Education; the 1966 International Covenant on Economic, Social and Cultural Rights; the 1981 Convention on the Elimination of All Forms of Discrimination against Women; and the 2006 Convention on the Rights of Persons with Disabilities.

[12]   According to a 1958 UNESCO convention, a person who is literate is one "who can, with understanding, both read and write a short, simple statement on his or her everyday life" (UNESCO 1958, p.153). Two decades later, UNESCO recommended a definition of functional literacy: "A person is functionally literate who can engage in all those activities in which literacy is required for effective functioning of his or her group and community and also for enabling him or her to continue to use reading, writing, and calculation for his or her own and the community's development" (UNESCO 1978, p.183).

Recent data puts simple literacy among those aged 15 and over at an average of 92.5% among member states, 5.3 percentage points higher than 2 decades ago. Gaps between ASEAN-6 and CLMV have narrowed in the past 2 decades in both adult and youth literacy, with average adult literacy among CLMV increasing by 6.7 percentage points from 2000 to 2019 compared to 4.3 percentage points among ASEAN in the same period. Youth literacy in CLMV also rose by 6.3 percentage points in 2000 to 2019, compared to 0.85 percentage points in ASEAN-6.

### Table 9: Select Literacy Indicators, 2000–2019

| ASEAN Member State | Proportion of Population Aged 15 Years and Above Achieving at Least a Fixed Level of Proficiency in Functional Literacy Skill (%) | | Adult Literacy Rate (percent of population 15 and over) | | Youth Literacy Rate (percent of youth aged 15–24) | |
|---|---|---|---|---|---|---|
| | 2016 | 2019 | 2000 | 2019 | 2000 | 2019 |
| Brunei Darussalam | 96.9 | 97.1[a] | 92.7[b] | 97.2[a] | 98.9[b] | 99.7[a] |
| Cambodia | 84.4 | 82.5[c] | 73.6[d] | 80.5[e] | 83.4[d] | 92.2[e] |
| Indonesia | 95.4 | 96.0[f] | 90.4[d] | 96.0[f] | 98.7[d] | 99.8[f] |
| Lao PDR | 84.7 | 70.4[c] | 69.6 | 84.7[e] | 80.6 | 92.5[e] |
| Malaysia | 94.9 | 95.0 | 88.7 | 95.0 | 97.2 | 96.8 |
| Myanmar | 88.9 | | 89.9 | 89.1 | 94.6 | 95.4 |
| Philippines | 90.3 | 91.6 | 92.6 | 96.3 | 95.1 | 98.4 |
| Singapore | 97.0 | 97.1[f] | 92.5 | 97.1[f] | 99.5 | 99.7[f] |
| Thailand | | 93.8[c] | 92.6 | 93.8[a] | 98.0 | 98.1[a] |
| Viet Nam | 95.0 | 95.1[f] | 90.2 | 95.8 | 94.8 | 98.6 |

ASEAN = Association of Southeast Asian Nations, Lao PDR = Lao People's Democratic Republic.
Notes: [a] Latest data from 2018.
[b] Latest data from 2001.
[c] Latest data from 2017.
[d] Latest data from 2004.
[e] Latest data from 2015.
[f] Latest data from 2020.
Source: ASEAN Statistics Division. 2018. ASEANstats Database on SDG Indicators. https://data.aseanstats.org/sdg (accessed 17 August 2022); UNESCO Institute for Statistics. Data for the Sustainable Development Goals. http://uis.unesco.org/ (accessed 17 August 2022).

Literacy is even higher for the youth aged 15–24, averaging 97% among ASEAN member states in recent years, compared to those aged 25 and over (which averages 92.6% in ASEAN member states in the same period). When data are broken down by gender, literacy is higher among males than females, except in the Philippines. Literacy rates have risen given increasing investments in schooling and other learning environments, although it is expected that the lockdowns have had repercussions to providing access to school participation, and to quality learning for all.

Early childhood education is an important determinant of achievements at later stages of education. Since 2000, preprimary net enrollment rates have risen in all ASEAN member states for which data is available (Table 10). The Lao PDR has achieved the most across member states in increasing preprimary net enrollment rates by as much as 9.3% per year. This impressive performance has been followed by Cambodia (8.2%) and the Philippines (6.2%), which have increased enrollment rates by more than 6% per year. Despite such improvements made in ASEAN, there remain large differences in enrollment rates in early childhood education across member states, with participation higher in ASEAN-6, though the gap has reduced. Recent data show Singapore has the highest level of preprimary enrollment in the ASEAN, with 96.1% of children in the 3–6 age bracket enrolled in preschool as of 2020. Preschool enrollment rates are below 50% in Myanmar (8.5% in 2018), Cambodia (33.6% in 2021), and the Lao PDR (49.3% in 2021).

**Table 10: Participation in Preprimary, Primary, Lower Secondary, Upper Secondary, and Tertiary Education, 2000–2021**

| ASEAN Member State | Gross Enrollment Rate in Preprimary Education (%) | | Net Enrollment Rate in Primary Education (%) | | Net Enrollment Rate in Lower Secondary Education (%) | | Net Enrollment Rate in Upper Secondary Education (%) | | Gross Enrollment Rate in Tertiary Educaton (%) | |
|---|---|---|---|---|---|---|---|---|---|---|
| | 2000 | 2021 | 2000 | 2021 | 2000 | 2021 | 2000 | 2021 | 2000 | 2021 |
| Brunei Darussalam | 46.9 | 63.5[a] | 99.0[b] | 98.3[a] | 99.7[b] | 99.7[a] | 86.4[b] | 69.6[a] | 12.7 | 32.0[a] |
| Cambodia | 6.4 | 33.6 | 93.2 | 86.5 | 14.5 | 81.7 | 16.8 | 56.0 | 2.5 | 13.0 |
| Indonesia | 24.1 | 62.3[c] | 96.2[d] | 94.4[c] | 72.1[b] | 83.7[c] | 40.0[d] | 77.5[c] | 14.9 | 36.3[c] |
| Lao PDR | 7.6 | 49.3 | 75.9[d] | 92.3 | 71.1 | 67.6 | 44.6 | 49.6 | 2.7 | 13.0 |
| Malaysia | 52.0 | 87.5 | 98.4 | 98.4[a] | 93.0 | 88.8[a] | 57.3 | 60.9 | 25.6 | 42.6[a] |
| Myanmar | 4.4[e] | 8.5[c] | 89.7 | 98.1[c] | 43.6 | 79.0[c] | 32.0 | 57.3[c] | 10.9[d] | 18.8[c] |
| Philippines | 25.4 | 90.2 | 90.6[d] | 91.2 | 86.8[d] | 87.9 | 66.4 | 78.4 | 30.4[d] | 35.5 |
| Singapore | | 96.1[a] | | 99.9[a] | | 99.1[a] | | 98.9[a] | | 93.1[a] |
| Thailand | | 74.0 | 98.9[e] | 99.7[f] | 95.7[e] | 93.3[j] | 46.2[e] | 68.2 | 34.9 | 43.8 |
| Viet Nam | 40.8 | 92.4 | 98.4[e] | 98.5 | 85.2 | | 50.5 | | 9.5 | 35.4 |

ASEAN = Association of Southeast Asian Nations, Lao PDR = Lao People's Democratic Republic.
Notes:  [a] Latest data from 2020
 [b] Latest data from 2005.
 [c] Latest data from 2018.
 [d] Latest data from 2001.
 [e] Latest data from 2005.
 [f] Latest data from 2022.
Sources: Net enrollment rates from UNESCO Institute for Statistics. Data for the Sustainable Development Goals. http://uis.unesco.org/ (accessed 4 September 2022); Gross enrollment rates from World Bank. World Bank Open Data. https://data.worldbank.org/ (accessed 4 September 2022).

With the global push for universal primary education, the ASEAN community has made substantial progress toward universal primary enrollment since 2000. The Lao PDR has had the greatest increase in primary participation at 1% per year. Disparities in primary enrollment rates across member states are not as wide as for other tiers of education, but nonetheless exist (especially as public spending for primary education varies in ASEAN member states). Gaps between ASEAN-6 and CLMV in primary school participation have, however, narrowed with the ratio of the average participation rates reducing from 1.08 in 2000 to 1.03 in 2021 (for economies with data in both years). Six member states have attained primary participation rates at 95% or more. Net enrollment rates in primary education are below 95% in Indonesia (94.4%), the Lao PDR (92.3%), the Philippines (91.2%), and Cambodia (86.5%). From 2000 to 2021, declines in primary school participation have been recorded in Cambodia and Indonesia.

Secondary school net enrollment rates for both lower and upper secondary levels have increased in nearly all ASEAN member states since 2000, with the largest increase in annual growth rates recorded in Cambodia (8.6% and 5.9% for lower and upper secondary levels, respectively). Indonesia also had nearly 5% increase per year in upper secondary participation rates, and a more modest increase in lower secondary participation. For the lower secondary level, an increase was also observed in the Lao PDR and the Philippines (aside from Cambodia and Indonesia), while for the upper secondary level, Brunei Darussalam's net enrollment regressed from 86.4% in 2005 to 69.6% in 2020. Recent data put Brunei Darussalam and Singapore as achieving near-universal lower secondary school participation, with Singapore also achieving near-universal upper secondary school participation. Meanwhile, upper secondary school net enrollment rates are below 50% in the Lao PDR (49.6%). Gaps in participation between ASEAN-6 and CLMV at the secondary level have narrowed. The ratio of the average participation rates dropped from 2.08 in 2000 to 1.19 in 2021 for the lower secondary level, and from 1.90 in 2000 to 1.31 in 2021 (for member states with data in both years).

Tertiary education in ASEAN member states have generally made progress since 2000 in increasing gross enrollment rates. Cambodia and the Lao PDR have gross enrollment rates that have gone up by about five times from 2000 to 2021. Viet Nam has also increased gross enrollment by more than three times from its rate which, like Cambodia and the Lao PDR, was below 10% in 2000. Brunei Darussalam also more than doubled its enrollment from 12.7% in 2000 to 32.0% in 2020. Gaps between ASEAN-6 and CLMV in tertiary education, like other education tiers, have also reduced with the ratio of the average gross enrollment rates decreasing from 3.7 in 2000 to 1.9 in 2021 (for member states with data in both years).

Although education indicators examined in this report suggest improvements in literacy and in access to education, the bigger challenge facing ASEAN member states, especially many in CLMV and the Philippines, is on attaining quality education for all (Box 1). This challenge has been further exacerbated by pandemic-induced school closures that have affected poor people and girls disproportionately.

## Box 1: Unintended Consequence of School Closures: Worsening Learning Poverty and Expected Earning Losses

Recent data on the Sustainable Development Goal 4 indicators on proficiency in reading and mathematics among learners in basic education across the Association of Southeast Asian Nations (ASEAN) member states show that in Cambodia, the Lao People's Democratic Republic, and Myanmar, as well as in the Philippines, less than one-fifth of students are learning minimum proficiency skills.

Learning poverty measures, developed by the World Bank and the United Nations Educational, Scientific and Cultural Organization, that account for both learning deficits as well as schooling deficits, are provided in the table. Singapore is way ahead in ASEAN with a learning poverty rate of 3%. Thailand and Viet Nam have rates at around 20%–25%. Meanwhile, Cambodia, the Lao People's Democratic Republic, Myanmar, and the Philippines have learning poverty rates at around 90% or more.

### Table: Learning Poverty Data in ASEAN Member States

| ASEAN Member State | Share of Children at the End-of-Primary Age Below Minimum Reading Proficiency Adjusted by Out-of-School Children (%) | | | |
| --- | --- | --- | --- | --- |
| | Male | Female | Both Sexes | Year |
| Cambodia | 93 | 88 | 90 | 2015 |
| Indonesia | 55 | 51 | 53 | 2019 |
| Lao PDR | 98 | 97 | 98 | 2019 |
| Malaysia | 50 | 35 | 43 | 2019 |
| Myanmar | | | 89 | 2019 |
| Philippines | 92 | 89 | 90 | 2019 |
| Singapore | 4 | 2 | 3 | 2016 |
| Thailand | 26 | 21 | 23 | 2011 |
| Viet Nam | | | 20 | 2019 |

ASEAN = Association of Southeast Asian Nations, Lao PDR = Lao People's Democratic Republic.
World Bank. Learning Poverty Global Database: Historical Data And Sub-Components. https://datacatalog.worldbank.org/search/dataset/0038947 (accessed 17 August 2022).

Data from the 2018 Program for International Student Assessment show that a country's spending on education per student is positively correlated with learning outcomes, proxied by average reading scores. The lack of investments in educational systems has thus had serious repercussions to the quality of learning.

*continued on the next page*

*Box 1 continued*

Learning losses that have taken place even before the pandemic have been substantial in several ASEAN member states, but these losses have been further worsened given school closures during the pandemic that have considerably affected poor people and girls disproportionately (ADB 2021; ADB 2022). In a special report, ADB (2022b) estimates that foregone learning due to the coronavirus disease school closures is estimated to have reached, on average, 0.83 learning-adjusted years of schooling (LAYS) for ASEAN. School closures up to October are estimated to have led to foregone learning equivalent to 10% of the average LAYS in ASEAN before the onset of the pandemic. Expected losses in future earnings are equivalent to 5% of pre-pandemic earnings for the region. Furthermore, gender gaps in absolute foregone learning are small in ASEAN, with males having 0.65 LAYS losses against 0.66 LAYS losses for females. However, since labor markets place a higher premium on the education of girls than that of boys, the expected losses in girls' future earnings are 26% higher than for boys in ASEAN.

In ASEAN member states, learning losses for the poorest quintile of learners are projected to be 31%, on average, higher than for counterparts among the richest quintile of students in their economy. Learners from the poorest quintile in ASEAN member states are expected to lose 0.92 LAYS, on average, equivalent to a 10.8% decline in average LAYS, while students from the richest quintile within the same economy are expected to lose 0.70 LAYS, on average, equivalent to an 8.2% decline. Wealth gaps in foregone learning are expected to translate into wealth gaps in earning losses—the poorest quintile of students is expected to lose 44% more than the richest quintile of students within the same economy in ASEAN.

Molato-Gayares et al. (2022) suggest that countries adopt strategies for recovering from learning losses amid the pandemic, including accurately determining the extent of knowledge losses, tailoring teaching based on student's learning levels, focusing on foundational skills, and providing quality in-service teacher training.

Sources: ADB. 2022. *Falling Further Behind: The Cost of COVID-19 School Closures by Gender and Wealth: Special Topic of the Asian Development Outlook 2021*. Manila. https://www.adb.org/sites/default/files/publication/784041/ado2022-learning-losses.pdf; ADB. 2021. *Learning and Earning Losses from COVID-19 School Closures in Developing Asia: Special Topic of the Asian Development Outlook 2021*. Manila. https://www.adb.org/sites/default/files/publication/692111/ado2021-special-topic.pdf; R. A. Molato-Gayares et al. 2022. How to Recover Learning Losses from COVID-19 School Closures in Asia and the Pacific. *ADB Briefs*. No. 217. Manila: ADB. https://www.adb.org/sites/default/files/publication/808471/adb-brief-217-learning-losses-covid-19-school-closures.pdf.

# VIII. DIGITAL ACCESS AND SKILLS

The increased use of technologies of the Fourth Industrial Revolution, especially digital technologies, has undoubtedly transformed the way we live, work, and learn. Digital technologies can be powerful agents for good, but they can widen existing inequalities, bringing about digital divides across and within countries. Over the years, however, both the proportion of the population using the internet, and fixed internet broadband penetration (Figure 12) have risen in ASEAN, with the gaps between ASEAN-6 and CLMV reducing for both information and communication technology (ICT) indicators. In particular, the ratio of the average internet penetration in ASEAN-6 to that of CLMV has decreased from 84.50 in 2000 to 1.34 in 2021. Likewise, the ratio of the average proportion of the population covered by at least 4G mobile network has dropped from 12.18 in 2014 to 1.14 in 2020. Data here are sparse for 2012 and 2013.

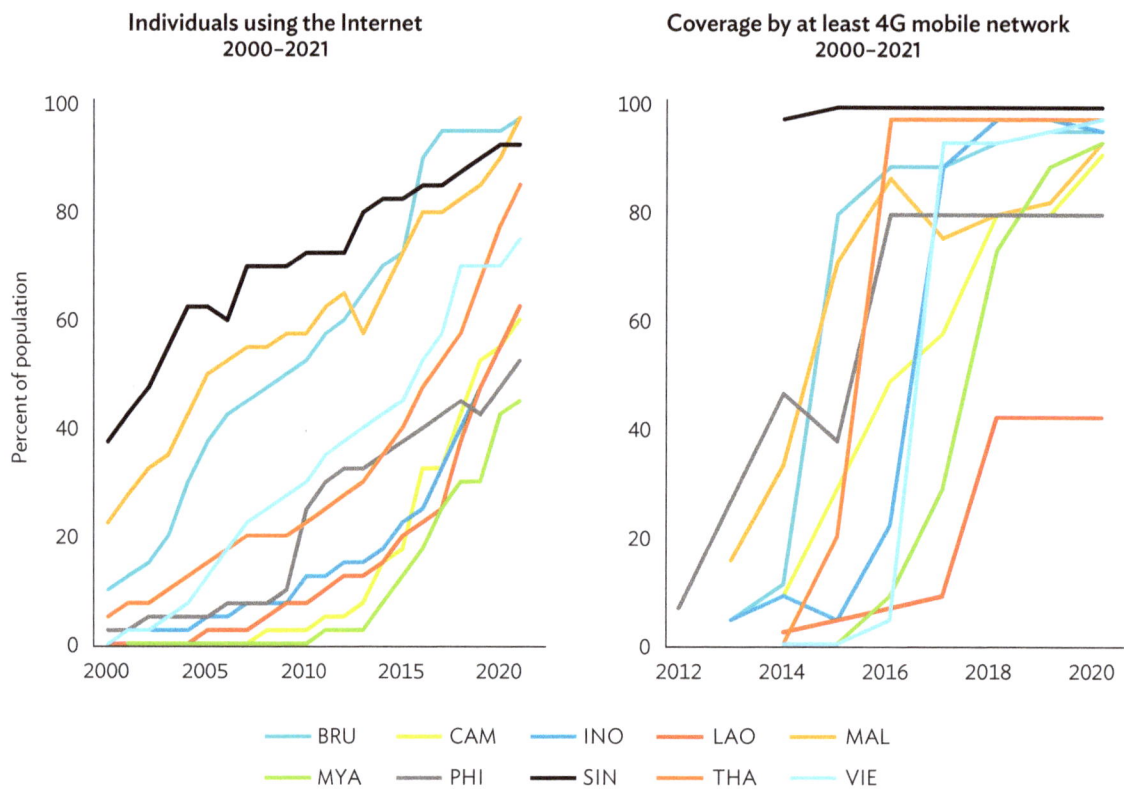

Figure 12: Individuals Using the Internet (2000–2021) and Proportion of Population Covered by at Least 4G Mobile Network (2012–2020)

BRU = Brunei Darussalam, CAM = Cambodia, INO = Indonesia, LAO = Lao People's Democratic Republic, MAL = Malaysia, MYA = Myanmar, PHI = Philippines, SIN = Singapore, THA = Thailand, VIE = Viet Nam.
Source: International Telecommunication Union (ITU). 2023. World Telecommunication/ICT Indicators Database. https://www.itu.int/en/ITU-D/Statistics/Pages/publications/wtid.aspx (accessed 20 March 2023).

Internet penetration averages 72.6% among ASEAN member states, as of 2021, an increase of about 64.5 percentage points from 2000. Internet access has increased much more in ASEAN-6, averaging as of 2021 at 81.1%, a rise of 68.8 percentage points from the 2000 penetration rate, compared to the average in CLMV at 60.1%, which rose from nearly zero (0.1%) in 2000. Internet use is more than 90% in Brunei Darussalam (98.1%) and Singapore (91.1%), while it is less than half of the population in Myanmar (44.0%). As of 2020, nearly all member states have at least 80% of their respective populations covered by at least 4G. The only exception is the Lao PDR where less than half (43.0%) are covered by at least 4G. In Singapore, coverage by at least 4G is universal.

Digital divides still persist among ASEAN member states, though they have narrowed considerably. These digital divides go beyond internet access and extend to digital skills. According to the Broadband Commission for Sustainable Development, digital skills are a "combination of behaviors, expertise, know-how, work habits, character traits, dispositions and critical understandings" (UNESCO 2017, p.4). In its *Digital Skills Assessment Guidebook*, the International Telecommunication Union (ITU 2018) discusses that digital skills are in a graduated continuum of proficiency levels—basic, intermediate, and advanced, with basic skills being part of life skills, while intermediate and advanced skills being the competencies useful in the work environment. Although, this typology of the International Telecommunication Union on proficiency levels is quite practical, it is also fluid—across time, what is considered "advanced" today can easily become "basic" tomorrow.

Recent data on digital skills among ASEAN member states also show a divide between ASEAN-6 and CLMV, and within member states, with skills in favor of richer member states such as Brunei Darussalam, Malaysia, and Singapore (Figure 13). These member states each lead in three out of nine digital skills measured for SDG Indicator 4.4.1 on the "proportion of youth and adults with ICT skills, by type of skills."

When compared with previous years, data in digital skills suggest very little changes in gaps between ASEAN-6 and CLMV. ASEAN member states should clearly make investments in improving digital access (by way of ICT infrastructure) and digital skills development. Those who lack access to digital technologies or the digital skills to navigate these technologies are at very strong risk of being sidelined and left behind in a world that is increasingly becoming more digital. The importance of digitalization has led ASEAN to come up with the ASEAN Digital Integration Index (ASEAN 2022a). Monitoring of this index is in line with the approach on the assessment of digital capabilities of ASEAN member states, in accordance with the ASEAN Digital Master Plan 2025 (ASEAN 2021c).

**Figure 13: Proportion of Youth and Adults with Information and Communication Technology Skills, by Digital Skill, Latest Year**

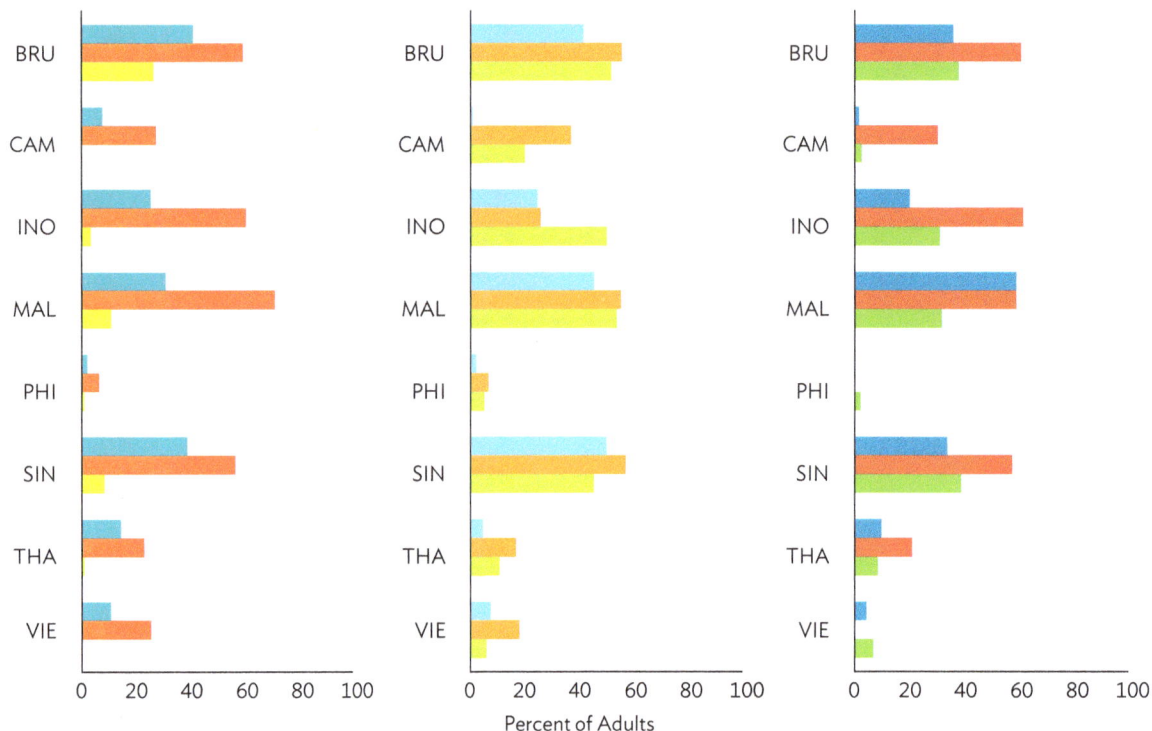

Percent of Adults

- ■ Using basic arithmetic formula in a spreadsheet
- ■ Using copy and paste tools to duplicate or move information within a document
- ■ Writing a computer program using a specialized programming language

- ■ Finding, downloading, installing and configuring software
- ■ Sending e-mails with attached files
- ■ Transferring files between a computer and other devices

- ■ Connecting and installing new devices
- ■ Copying or moving a file or folder
- ■ Creating electronic presentations with presentation software

BRU = Brunei Darussalam, CAM = Cambodia, ICT = information and communication technology, INO = Indonesia, MAL = Malaysia, PHI = Philippines, SIN = Singapore, THA = Thailand, VIE = Viet Nam.
Notes: [a] Three ICT skills listed in SDG 4.4.1 are not available for PHI.
    [b] Data covers youth and adults
    [c] The Lao PDR has generated data for men and for women (but not the total) for this indicator in the Lao Social Indicator Survey 2017.
Sources: United Nations Department of Economic and Social Affairs. 2021. SDG Global Database. https://unstats.un.org/sdgs/dataportal (accessed 17 August 2022); PHI-2019 data from Department of Information and Communications Technology (DICT). 2019. National ICT Household Survey 2019. https://dict.gov.ph/ictstatistics/nicths2019/ (accessed 17 August 2022).

# IX. GENDER EQUALITY

Gender equality means that everyone, regardless of gender, is provided equal rights, equitable opportunities, and fair treatment and protection so that they are empowered to reach their full potential. This entails both men and women being given equal opportunities to education, paid employment, and decision-making power in employment, whether in the private or public sector. If someone cannot access education or health services early on in life because of their gender or other circumstances of their birth, that ultimately creates a cost not only for that person concerned but also for everyone in terms of wasted human and economic potential.

In nearly all ASEAN member states, females and males are at par in youth literacy rate with the Gender Parity Index (GPI) for 2019 data averaging to 1.00, an increase of around 0.03 compared to data from 2000 (Table 11). On average, males were more literate than females in Cambodia and the Lao PDR in 2000, but recent data suggests that the gap has narrowed considerably. Similar trends can be observed in the GPI for gross enrollment rates, particularly at the secondary and tertiary levels—the advantage in access to education is among males in Cambodia and the Lao PDR, even in recent years, though the gap has narrowed. For tertiary education, access in half of member states has even been in favor of females.

### Table 11: Gender Parity Index for Indicators in Learning, 2000–2019

| | Gender Parity Index | | | | | | | |
| | Literacy Rate, Youth (ages 15–24) | | School Enrollment, Primary (gross) | | School Enrollment, Secondary (gross) | | School Enrollment, Tertiary (gross) | |
| ASEAN Member State | 2000–2009 | 2010–2019 | 2000–2009 | 2010–2019 | 2000–2009 | 2010–2019 | 2000–2009 | 2010–2019 |
|---|---|---|---|---|---|---|---|---|
| Brunei Darussalam | 1.00 | 1.00 | 0.96 | 1.00 | 1.00 | 1.02 | 1.44 | 1.41 |
| Cambodia | 0.94 | 1.01 | 0.92 | 0.96 | 0.69 | | 0.45 | 0.79 |
| Indonesia | 1.00 | 1.00 | 0.98 | 0.99 | 0.99 | 1.01 | 0.87 | 1.05 |
| Lao PDR | 0.87 | 0.91 | 0.87 | 0.95 | 0.75 | 0.89 | 0.65 | 0.93 |
| Malaysia | 1.00 | 1.00 | 1.00 | 1.01 | 1.10 | 1.07 | 1.22 | 1.22 |
| Myanmar | 0.98 | 1.00 | 0.99 | 0.97 | 0.97 | 1.07 | 1.26 | 1.24 |
| Philippines | 1.02 | 1.01 | 0.99 | 0.97 | 1.10 | 1.10 | 1.19 | 1.22 |
| Singapore | 1.00 | 1.00 | | 1.00 | | 0.99 | | 1.13 |
| Thailand | 1.00 | 1.00 | 0.98 | 0.99 | 1.05 | 1.02 | 1.14 | 1.25 |
| Viet Nam | 0.99 | 1.00 | 0.96 | 1.00 | | | 0.86 | 1.03 |

ASEAN = Association of Southeast Asian Nations, Lao PDR = Lao People's Democratic Republic.
Source: UNESCO Institute for Statistics. Data for the Sustainable Development Goals. http://uis.unesco.org/ (accessed 30 August 2022).

The gap in the average GPI between ASEAN-6 and CLMV has not been wide for literacy rates among the young and for primary school enrollment, and these gaps have further narrowed over the years. The ratio of the average gender gap in literacy rates of ASEAN-6 to CLMV has fallen from 1.06 in 2000–2009 to 1.02 from 2010 to 2019. Further, the corresponding ratios for primary school have also dropped from 1.05 to 1.02. For secondary and tertiary enrollment, the gaps in average GPIs between ASEAN-6 and CLMV have also narrowed, with the corresponding ratios decreasing from 1.22 to 1.07, and from 1.46 to 1.23, respectively.

Through its gender gap indices, the World Economic Forum (WEF) has also provided another lens on the diversity of experience across ASEAN member states in attaining gender equality. Since 2006, the WEF has listed the Philippines as the best performer in gender outcomes in the ASEAN community, with a global ranking among the top 20 (Table 12).

**Table 12: Rank in Global Gender Gap Index of ASEAN Member States, 2017–2022**

| Member State | 2017 | | 2018 | | 2020 | | 2021 | | 2022 |
|---|---|---|---|---|---|---|---|---|---|
| Brunei Darussalam | 102 | ↑ | 90 | ↓ | 95 | ↓ | 111 | ↑ | 104 |
| Cambodia | 99 | ↑ | 93 | ↑ | 89 | ↓ | 103 | ↑ | 45 |
| Indonesia | 84 | ↓ | 85 | → | 85 | ↓ | 101 | ↑ | 92 |
| Lao PDR | 64 | ↑ | 26 | ↓ | 43 | ↑ | 36 | ↓ | 53 |
| Malaysia | 104 | ↑ | 101 | ↓ | 104 | ↓ | 112 | ↑ | 103 |
| Myanmar | 83 | ↓ | 88 | ↓ | 114 | ↑ | 109 | ↑ | 106 |
| Philippines | 10 | ↑ | 8 | ↓ | 16 | ↓ | 17 | ↓ | 19 |
| Singapore | 65 | ↓ | 67 | ↑ | 54 | → | 54 | ↑ | 49 |
| Thailand | 75 | ↑ | 73 | ↓ | 75 | ↓ | 79 | → | 79 |
| Viet Nam | 69 | ↓ | 77 | ↓ | 87 | → | 87 | ↑ | 83 |

ASEAN = Association of Southeast Asian Nations, Lao PDR = Lao People's Democratic Republic.
Notes: In the Global Gender Gap Index, the lower the rank the better the performance.
    Green arrows pointing up : mean improved performance toward closing the gender gap
    Red arrows pointing down: mean reduced performance toward closing the gender gap
    Orange arrows going sideways: mean no change in closing the gender gap
Source: World Economic Forum (WEF). 2021. The Global Gender Gap Report 2022. https://www.weforum.org/reports/global-gender-gap-report-2022 (accessed 30 August 2022).

While the Philippines fares better than most ASEAN member states in gender equality (not only from the WEF indices but also among other international assessments), stubborn glass ceilings persist in women representation in top-level decision-making positions. The Beijing Declaration and Platform for Action identified women in power and decision-making as a critical area of concern. Table 13 shows that ASEAN member states are far from achieving gender parity in national parliament. ASEAN-6 has had fewer women in parliament in early years compared to CLMV, though the gap between ASEAN-6 and CLMV has narrowed in recent years, with little changes in the proportion of women in parliament across CLMV. Further, across ASEAN member states, some progress has been made in increasing female leaders in the business community. Only the Philippines has had more than half of managerial positions occupied by women.

**Table 13: Indicators on Women Leaders, 2000–2022**

| ASEAN Member State | Proportion of Seats Held by Women in National Parliaments (%) | | | Proportion of Women in Managerial Positions (%) | | |
|---|---|---|---|---|---|---|
| | 2000–2009 | 2010–2019 | 2020–2022 | 2000–2009 | 2010–2019 | 2020–2022 |
| Brunei Darussalam | | 9.1 | 9.1 | 25.7 | 36.1 | 36.5 |
| Cambodia | 10.5 | 20.5 | 20.8 | 18.2 | 26.6 | |
| Indonesia | 9.7 | 18.4 | 21.1 | 20.1 | 26.2 | 32.5 |
| Lao PDR | 23.1 | 25.8 | 25.7 | | 45.4 | |
| Malaysia | 9.7 | 10.7 | 14.8 | 23.6 | 22.6 | 24.9 |
| Myanmar | | 7.5 | 13.9 | | 33.0 | |
| Philippines | 16.4 | 25.9 | 27.9 | 57.1 | 50.1 | 53.0 |
| Singapore | 15.6 | 23.7 | 27.5 | 28.2 | 34.5 | 37.6 |
| Thailand | 9.4 | 10.1 | 15.9 | 26.7 | 31.2 | 39.2 |
| Viet Nam | 26.6 | 25.3 | 27.9 | 19.8 | 24.9 | 25.8 |

ASEAN = Association of Southeast Asian Nations, Lao PDR = Lao People's Democratic Republic.
Sources: Inter-Parliamentary Union. Historical Data on Women in National Parliaments. https://data.ipu.org/historical-women (accessed 14 August 2022); United Nations Department of Economic and Social Affairs. 2021. SDG Global Database. https://unstats.un.org/sdgs/dataportal (accessed 8 August 2022).

# X. LIVING CONDITIONS

Everyone has a right to decent living conditions. Human rights treaties such as the Convention on the Elimination of All Forms of Discrimination against Women and the Convention on the Rights of Persons with Disabilities explicitly refer to the basic right to enjoy adequate living conditions in relation to housing, sanitation, electricity, and water supply. In 2010, the UN General Assembly recognized access to safe and clean drinking water and safe sanitation as a human right, and called for international efforts and partnerships to help countries provide safe, clean, accessible, and affordable drinking water and sanitation. Targets 6.1 and 6.2 of the SDGs, respectively, call for universal and equitable access to safe and affordable drinking water for all, and for adequate and equitable sanitation for all. Meanwhile, SDG Target 11.1 aims to ensure access for all to adequate, safe, and affordable housing and basic services, and upgrade slums, whereas SDG Target 7.1 works to ensure universal access to affordable, reliable, and modern energy services. Frameworks on multidimensional poverty (of UNDP and the World Bank) include indicators and a dimension on living conditions since drinking water, sanitation, housing, and electricity are fundamental determinants of welfare and human development outcomes, such as people's health and childhood development.

ASEAN, especially CLMV, has made progress in improving living standards across the years since 2000 (Table 14), with the development gap between ASEAN-6 and CLMV in urban housing, safe water, and safe sanitation reduced in 2000–2020. Three out of four in CLMV—Cambodia, the Lao PDR, and Myanmar—have made considerable progress in reducing the proportion of their respective urban populations living in slums, informal settlements, or inadequate housing facilities, as well as in increasing access to safe drinking water services and to electricity (from their baseline levels 1.5 to 2 decades ago). Thus CLMV has caught up to ASEAN-6 in urban housing, with the average proportion of urban residents in inadequate housing in ASEAN-6 relative to CLMV increasing from 0.57 in 2000 to 0.98 in 2018.

## Table 14: Select Living Standard Indicators, 2000–2020

| ASEAN Member State | Proportion of Urban Population Living in Slums, Informal Settlements, or Inadequate Housing Facilities (%) | | Access of Population to Safely Managed Drinking Water Services (%) | | Access of Population to Safely Managed Sanitation Services (%) | | Access of Population to Electricity (%) | |
|---|---|---|---|---|---|---|---|---|
| | 2000 | 2018 | 2000 | 2020 | 2000 | 2020 | 2000 | 2020 |
| Brunei Darussalam | | | | | 96.3[a] | 96.3[b] | 100.0 | 100.0 |
| Cambodia | 78.9[c] | 45.6 | 17.0 | 28.0 | 38.0 | 86.5 | 16.6 | 86.4 |
| Indonesia | 34.4 | 30.4 | | | 9.8 | 68.8 | 86.3 | 97.0 |
| Lao PDR | 79.3[c] | 18.5 | 5.0 | 18.0 | 28.2 | 79.5 | 42.5 | 100.0 |
| Malaysia | | | 93.0 | 94.0 | 63.5 | 73.6 | 99.1 | 100.0 |
| Myanmar | 45.6[c] | 57.1 | 27.0 | 59.0 | | | 41.8 | 70.4 |
| Philippines | 47.2 | 44.3 | 36.0 | 47.0 | 61.1 | 82.3 | 74.7 | 96.8 |
| Singapore | | | 100.0 | 100.0 | 100.0 | 100.0 | 100.0 | 100.0 |
| Thailand | 26.0[c] | 24.5 | | | 92.4 | 98.7 | 82.1 | 100.0 |
| Viet Nam | 48.8 | 13.5 | | | 51.9 | 89.2 | 87.8 | 100.0 |

ASEAN = Association of Southeast Asian Nations, Lao PDR = Lao People's Democratic Republic.
Notes: [a] Latest data from 2007.
   [b] Latest data from 2015.
   [c] Latest data from 2005.
Source: United Nations Department of Economic and Social Affairs. 2021. SDG Global Database. https://unstats.un.org/sdgs/dataportal (accessed 13 October 2022).

The Lao PDR (79.3%) and Cambodia (78.9%), which, in 2005, had four-fifths of their urban populations residing in non-decent housing, have significantly reduced these populations by 2018 at an annual rate of 5.9% and 3.2%, respectively. Meanwhile, Viet Nam (48.8%), the Philippines (47.2%), and Myanmar (45.6%), which had about half of their urban populations living in slums, informal settlements, or inadequate housing facilities, had made respectively substantial progress, modest progress, or regressions in reducing their urban slum population. Indonesia, the Philippines, and Thailand have made modest progress in reducing their percentage of urban residents in slums, informal settlements, or inadequate housing facilities.

Myanmar (32.0), the Lao PDR (13.0), Cambodia (11.0), and the Philippines (11.0) have increased their access to safe drinking water services by over 10 percentage points from 2000 to 2020. Thus, the average proportion of people with access to safe water in ASEAN-6 relative to CLMV has reduced from 4.90 in 2000 to 2.48 in 2020. During the same period, Indonesia (58.8) and the Lao PDR (51.2) have increased access to safe sanitation by over 50 percentage points. This is followed by Cambodia, Viet Nam, and the Philippines that have increased access to safe sanitation services by at least 20 percentage points. The development gaps in safe sanitation between ASEAN-6 and CLMV has reduced with the average access to safe sanitation in ASEAN-6 relative to CLMV decreasing from 1.91 in 2000 to 0.97 in 2020.

Cambodia, the Lao PDR, and Myanmar have the best performance in increasing access to electricity across ASEAN member states, with the Lao PDR attaining near universal access. Thus, electricity access in ASEAN-6 relative to CLMV has dropped from 2.06 in 2000 to 1.11 in 2020. Access to electricity is nearing universal in the ASEAN community, with nearly all but two member states providing access to more than 95% of their respective populations, as of the latest data. The only exceptions are Cambodia (86.4%) and Myanmar (70.4%), which have increased access to electricity from 2000 to 2020 by as much as 69.8 and 28.6 percentage points, respectively. Electricity access in Myanmar, however, is, still substantially much lower in rural (57.5%) than in urban (92.7%) areas.

# XI. SOCIAL SAFETY NETS

Social protection, particularly social safety nets, is a mechanism to prevent poor people from being caught in a poverty trap and to assist other vulnerable sectors of society from falling into poverty when they are affected by shocks, such as disasters, inflationary pressures, or economic downturn (ADB 2022a). Social safety nets provide temporary assistance to households for strengthening their resilience to effects of idiosyncratic and macroeconomic stress on their welfare conditions. According to the World Bank, before the COVID-19 pandemic, more than a third of the world's extremely poor escapes extreme poverty because of social safety nets: adequate social protection systems are correlated with improved social mobility (World Bank 2018). In ASEAN member states, about a third (35.7%) of their populations are covered by at least one social protection benefit, with the coverage generally better in ASEAN-6 compared to CLMV (Box 2).

Latest data from 2014 to 2019 (compared to data mostly for years 2006 to 2009) on coverage in the population by type of social protection program in ASEAN member states, sourced from the World Bank's Atlas of Social Protection Indicators of Resilience and Equity database, is provided in Table 15. Eight ASEAN member states have data available on coverage on social insurance programs, while social assistance coverage data is available for seven ASEAN member states. Recent World Bank's Atlas of Social Protection Indicators of Resilience and Equity data on coverage of social insurance ranges between 1.9% (in Cambodia) to 15.2% (in Viet Nam). Thailand had a drop in social insurance coverage, reporting a difference of 11 percentage points from its 2006 data (14.7%). As a result, the gap between ASEAN-6 and CLMV has reduced from early years to latest years.

**Table 15: Select Social Safety Net Indicators, 2008–2016**

| ASEAN Member State | Proportion of Population (%) Covered by | | | | | |
|---|---|---|---|---|---|---|
| | Social Insurance Programs | | Social Assistance Programs | | Labor Market Programs | |
| | 2008 | 2016 | 2008 | 2016 | 2008 | 2016 |
| Brunei Darussalam | … | … | … | … | … | … |
| Cambodia | 2.6 | 1.9 | … | 20.9 | 1.2[a] | … |
| Indonesia | 9.3[b] | 10.9[c] | 40.9[a] | 29.2[c] | 1.4[a] | 9.1[c] |
| Lao PDR | 1.7[d] | 2.2[e] | … | … | … | … |
| Malaysia | 6.8 | 8.4 | 82.8 | 75.7 | … | … |
| Myanmar | … | 5.3[f] | … | 8.7[f] | … | 2.3[f] |
| Philippines | 7.5[a] | 8.9[g] | … | 33.8[g] | … | … |
| Singapore | … | … | … | … | … | … |
| Thailand | 14.7[h] | 3.6[c] | 43.3[h] | 74.1[c] | … | … |
| Viet Nam | 17.2[h] | 15.2[b] | 22.5[h] | 17.5[b] | 6.1[a] | 9.0[b] |

ASEAN = Association of Southeast Asian Nations, Lao PDR = Lao People's Democratic Republic.
Notes: [a] 2009; [b] 2014; [c] 2019; [d] 2007; [e] 2018; [f] 2017; [g] 2015; [h] 2006.
Source: World Bank. 2013. Atlas of Social Protection: Indicators of Resilience and Equity (ASPIRE). World Bank: Washington, DC. https://www.worldbank.org/en/data/datatopics/aspire (accessed 24 November 2022).

Among ASEAN member states, Thailand has been the most successful in increasing the proportion of the population provided with social assistance, with a 30.8-percentage-point increase from 43.3% in 2006, thus bringing coverage to 74.1% in 2019. Aside from Thailand, Malaysia also has about three out of every four persons benefiting from social assistance, but coverages of social assistance in Cambodia, Myanmar, and

Viet Nam is only about a fifth or less of the respective populations. The Philippines also reports an increase on social assistance coverage by 6.5 percentage points in 2 years, from 27.4% in 2013 (with the expansion of its conditional cash transfer program). On the other hand, three ASEAN member states have had a decline in coverage of social assistance—Indonesia by 11.8 percentage points, Malaysia by 7.1 percentage points, and Viet Nam by 5.0 percentage points. Social assistance data are sparse to compare ASEAN-6 with CLMV. Data on coverage for labor market programs is even more limited, as there are only two ASEAN member states with at least two data points. Indonesia reported an improvement of 7.7 percentage points in 10 years from 1.4% in 2009.

---

**Box 2: A Third of Populations in ASEAN Member States Covered by At Least One Social Protection Benefit**

Target 1.3 of Sustainable Development Goal (SDG) 1 on "zero poverty" is "Implement nationally appropriate social protection systems and measures for all, including floors, and by 2030 achieve substantial coverage of the poor and the vulnerable." One of the global SDG indicators for monitoring this target is SDG Indicator 1.3.1, referring to "the proportion of population covered by social protection floors or systems, by sex, distinguishing children, unemployed persons, older persons, persons with disabilities, pregnant women, newborns, work-injury victims and the poor and the vulnerable."

The latest available data in the Asian Development Bank's Key Indicators Database show that Association of Southeast Asian Nations member states had about a third (35.7%) of their population covered by at least one social protection benefit (Figure).

**Figure: Proportion of Population Covered by At Least One Social Protection Benefit, 2020** (%)

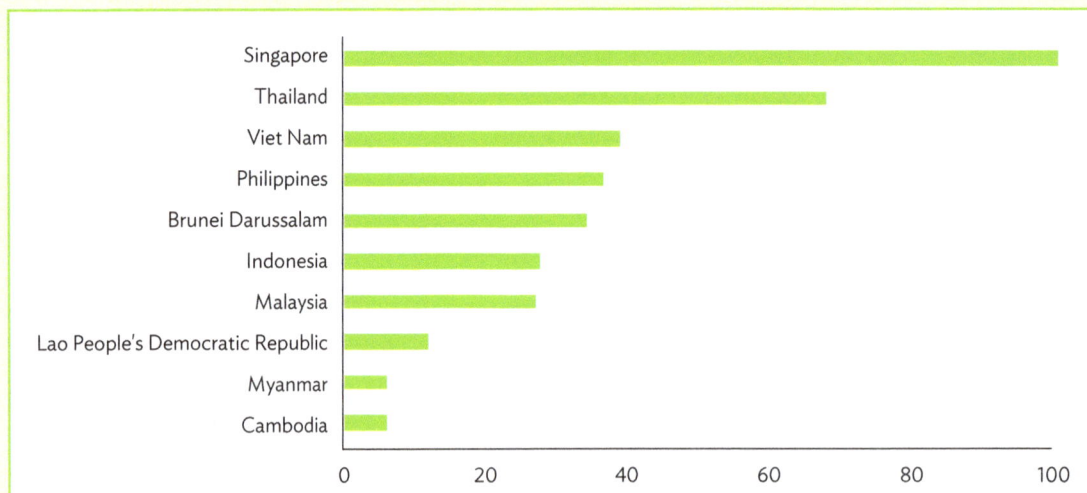

Source: Asian Development Bank (ADB). Asian Development Bank: Key Indicators Database Online. https://kidb.adb.org (accessed 17 August 2022).

Singapore achieved universal coverage of social protection, while Thailand covers roughly two-thirds of its population with a safety net. Meanwhile, at least a third of the population of Viet Nam, the Philippines, and Brunei Darussalam are covered with at least one social protection benefit. Cambodia, Myanmar, and the Lao People's Democratic Republic, however, have yet to cover at least a fifth of their respective populations with social protection. Before the coronavirus disease pandemic, some member states have been implementing conditional cash transfer programs, aside from increasing health insurance coverage. As the pandemic unfolded, governments ramped up social protection coverage to help poor and vulnerable groups cope with mobility restrictions that impacted their livelihoods and well-being. These measures came in the form of cash transfers, new unemployment programs, unemployment insurance, food subsidies, and sickness benefits.

# XII. ENVIRONMENT AND CLIMATE CHANGE

The ASEAN community faces persistent and emerging development challenges, including effects of climate change and disasters. Some ASEAN member states, such as Indonesia, Myanmar, and the Philippines have had a large number of deaths from disasters that are a consequence of hazards, exposure of people to the hazards, and vulnerabilities (Table 16). Consequently, ASEAN member states need to address these critical areas that risk undermining the development they have achieved collectively and individually.

**Table 16: Select Indicators on Effects of Disasters, 2005–2020**

| ASEAN Member State | Number of Deathes, Missing Persons, and Directly-Affected Persons Attributed to Climate-Related Disasters per 100,000 population | | | | | |
| | Deaths (per 100,000 population)* | | Directly-Affected Persons (per 100,000 population)* | | Missing Persons (per 100,000 population) | |
| | 2005–2012 | 2013–2020 | 2005–2012 | 2013–2020 | 2005–2012 | 2013–2020 |
|---|---|---|---|---|---|---|
| Cambodia | 132 | 130 | 109 | 179 | 1 | 1 |
| Indonesia | 1,746 | 3,546 | 435 | 875 | 1 | 1 |
| Lao PDR | 33 | | 1,285 | | 1 | |
| Malaysia | 23 | 73 | 89 | 569 | 0 | 0 |
| Myanmar | 17,363 | 330 | 5,402 | 777 | 35 | 1 |
| Philippines | 935 | 2,692 | 4,290 | 6,996 | 2 | 3 |
| Thailand | | 155 | | 149 | | 0 |
| Viet Nam | 384 | | 477 | | 1 | |

ASEAN = Association of Southeast Asian Nations, Lao PDR = Lao People's Democratic Republic.
Note: * indicate averages over the period.
Source: United Nations Department of Economic and Social Affairs. 2021. SDG Global Database. https://unstats.un.org/sdgs/dataportal (accessed 14 August 2022).

ASEAN-6 (on account of Indonesia and the Philippines) had more deaths than CLMV (except in early years, with the devastating effect in Myanmar due of cyclone Nargis in 2008). The number of persons directly affected by disasters in ASEAN-6 relative to CLMV remained relatively stable in both early and recent years, while the number of missing persons has dropped in ASEAN-6, with the corresponding magnitudes in CLMV remaining the same.

The growing intensity and effects of climate disasters are partly a result of humanity's relationship with the planet. As of 2020, only Thailand and Viet Nam have increased forest area as a proportion of total land area compared to baselines in 2000 (Table 17). Forest area as a percentage of total land area is a proxy of the extent to which the forests in a country are being conserved or restored, although it is only partly a measure for the extent to which they are sustainably managed. ASEAN-6 has reduced forest area by 2 percentage points, compared to CLMV's 5-percentage-point reduction in 2000–2020. In consequence, the advantage of CLMV's forest coverage to that of ASEAN-6 has reduced.

**Table 17: Select Indicators on Protecting the Environment, 2000–2021**

| ASEAN Member State | Ratio of Protected Area to Total Area and Forest Cover to Total Land Area | | Coverage of Protected Areas in Relation to Marine Areas |
|---|---|---|---|
| | 2000 | 2020 | 2021 |
| Brunei Darussalam | 75.3 | 72.1 | 0.6 |
| Cambodia | 61.1 | 45.7 | 1.4 |
| Indonesia | 53.9 | 49.1 | 2.9 |
| Lao PDR | 75.5 | 71.9 | 0.0 |
| Malaysia | 59.9 | 58.2 | 5.4 |
| Myanmar | 53.4 | 43.7 | 0.5 |
| Philippines | 24.5 | 24.1 | 3.6 |
| Singapore | 25.4 | 21.7 | 0.0 |
| Thailand | 37.2 | 38.9 | 4.3 |
| Viet Nam | 37.9 | 46.7 | 0.5 |

ASEAN = Association of Southeast Asian Nations, Lao PDR = Lao People's Democratic Republic.
Source: United Nations Department of Economic and Social Affairs. 2021. SDG Global Database. https://unstats.un.org/sdgs/dataportal (accessed 14 August 2022).

Further, none of ASEAN member states have conserved at least 10% of coastal and marine areas, as of 2021. The establishment of protected areas is an important mechanism for curtailing the decline in biodiversity and for ensuring sustainable use of marine natural resources. SDG Target 14.5 aims to conserve at least 10% of coastal and marine areas by 2020.

ASEAN people need to be empowered to tackle climate change with improved capacity and increased use of technology and innovation to prevent, prepare for, and recover from climate change and its climate disaster-related impacts, for instance, through active involvement in early warning systems, sustainable land and marine area ecosystem management, and access to disaster recovery products and services such as micro-insurance and crop insurance. Other critical actions include stronger environmental protection, more effective engagement in clean and renewable energy, and ensuring that everyone benefits from the expansion of green jobs, as well as the integration of social inclusion perspectives into climate finance.

# XIII. GOVERNANCE

Governance is the way authority and leadership are exercised in the management of economic and social resources for development. Many view governance as a determinant of economic, political, and social outcomes, and consequently, good governance is held to be an important ingredient for economic growth. This view stems from the recognition that institutions matter to development, and governance is ultimately about having institutions working for development.

Three measures of governance—Government Effectiveness Index, the Business Climate Change Index – Ease of doing business[13] score, and the Global Competitiveness Index—are highly correlated, whether for earliest or latest years data in 2000–2020 (Figure 14). Higher-income countries Singapore, Malaysia, and Brunei Darussalam tend to get high performance marks in these indices, while low-income countries Cambodia, the Lao PDR, and Myanmar tend to do poorly. Despite the correlation of these indices, the pattern in development gaps suggested by the indicators are not similar given the rate at which the indices are changing per ASEAN member state. For the Government Effectiveness Index, the gap between ASEAN-6 and CLMV has narrowed, but for the other two indicators, the gap between ASEAN-6 and CLMV has slightly widened. CLMV will have to benchmark their performance relative to ASEAN-6.

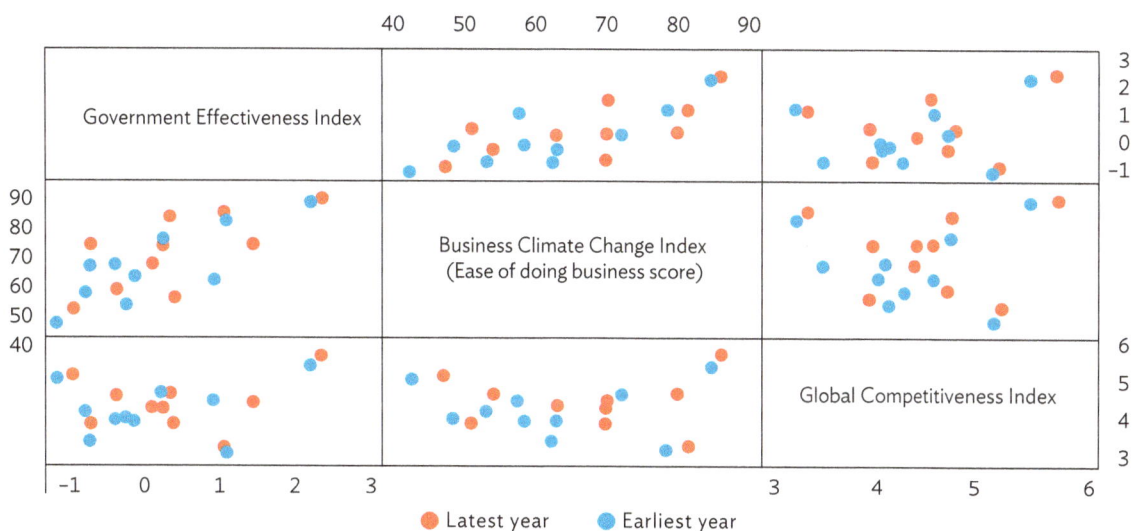

Figure 14: Performance of ASEAN Member States in Governance Indicators, Earliest and Latest Years, 2000–2020

ASEAN = Association of Southeast Asian Nations.
Sources: World Bank. Worldwide Governance Indicators. https://databank.worldbank.org/source/worldwide-governance-indicators (accessed 28 August 2022); World Bank. 2004. Doing Business Data. https://archive.doingbusiness.org/en/data (accessed 28 August 2022); Schwab, K. and S. Zahidi. 2020. Global competitiveness report: special edition 2020. World Economic Forum. https://www3.weforum.org/docs/WEF_TheGlobalCompetitivenessReport2020.pdf (accessed 28 August 2022).

---

[13] The World Bank has discontinued the Doing Business Report since September 2021 and is in the process of producing the Business Enabling Environment Index.

# XIV. OVERALL PROGRESS IN NARROWING THE DEVELOPMENT GAP

As shown in the previous sections of this report, the ASEAN community had mixed progress in narrowing the development gap with inequalities not always reducing within and across ASEAN member states. Differences across countries can be conceptually viewed from living standards or national welfare. GDP per capita has been traditionally used as the key proxy variable for measuring living standards, despite its limitations as a measure of national welfare (Stiglitz, Fitoussi, and Durand 2018). Typically, we can examine convergence or divergence in economic progress of countries, as reflected in GDP per capita.

Whether convergence in terms of GDP per capita is supported by theory has been a recurrent question of economic thinking. According to the early growth theories, economic integration was meant to allow for an equalization of growth rates while reducing the income gap. Thus, regardless of the difference in the initial state of economic development of ASEAN member states, economic progress may converge accordingly. While income differences among the member states persist, it is posited that a "catching up" to the richer economies by the relatively less developed is feasible. Several schools of thought, however, have argued that strong diverging forces might emerge among economies, supporting thus the existence of an opposite dynamic.

Two standard indicators are available in the economic literature: Beta-convergence and Sigma-convergence (Islam 2003). The concept of Beta-convergence implies that poor countries grow faster than rich countries. Typically, the existence of Beta-convergence is tested by regressing the growth in per capita GDP on its initial level for a given cross section of countries or regions within countries (Barro 1991). Convergence in the unconditional sense is implied, according to this methodology, if the coefficient on initial per capita GDP is negative and statistically significant.

From 2000 to 2019, we readily notice Beta-convergence in Figure 15. However, a structural break resulted with the onset of the pandemic, leading to a divergence as richer member states, particularly Singapore, recovering strong, whereas most ASEAN member states, especially Myanmar, have not reached pre-pandemic GDP per capita levels. Beta-convergence detects possible catching-up processes, while Sigma-convergence simply refers to a reduction of disparities among regions across time. While the two concepts are closely related, they are not equivalent. Beta-convergence is necessary, but not sufficient for Sigma-convergence. That is, economies can converge toward one another, but shocks can push them apart or because, in the case of conditional Beta-convergence, economies can converge toward different steady states.

An alternative methodology to a least squares regression for measuring Beta-convergence generally involves estimating a growth equation in the following form:

$$ln(\Delta y_{it}) = \alpha + (1+\beta)\, ln(y_{it-1}) + \gamma\, Z_{it} + \theta_i + \delta_t + u_{it}$$

using panel data, where

- $y_{it}$ and $\Delta y_{it}$ are respectively the level and growth rate of (log) GDP per capita in member state $l$ at time $t$;
- $Z_{it}$ are determinants of the growth rate;
- $u_{it}$ is a model error term; and
- $\alpha$, $\beta$, $\gamma$, $\theta$ and $\delta$ are parameters to be estimated.

**Figure 15: Beta-Convergence in Per Capital Gross Domestic Product in ASEAN, 2000–2019 and 2019–2021**

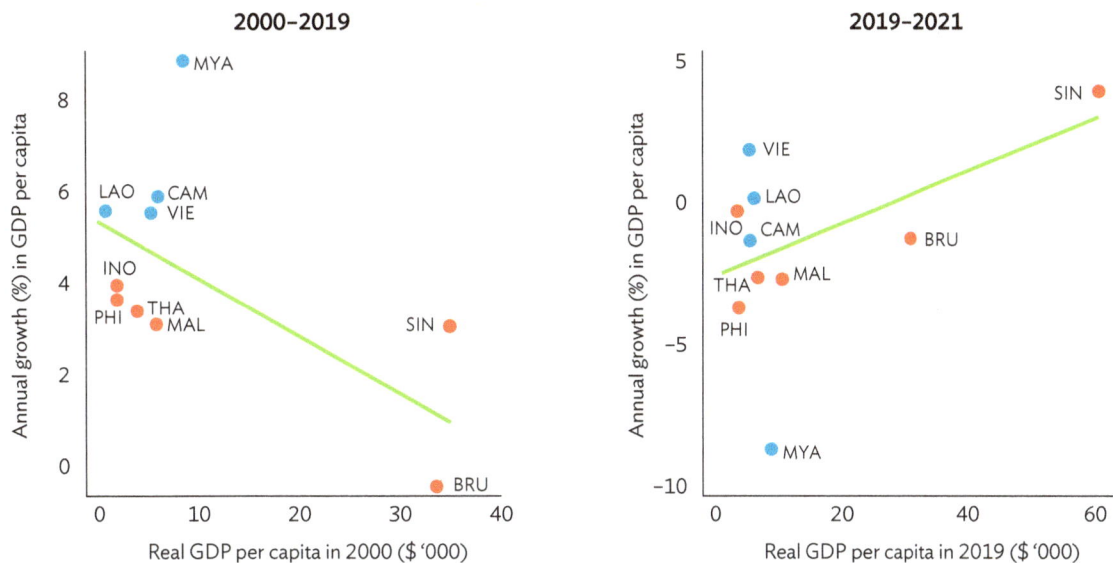

ASEAN = Association of Southeast Asian Nations, GDP = gross domestic product, BRU = Brunei Darussalam, CAM = Cambodia, INO = Indonesia, LAO = Lao People's Democratic Republic, MAL = Malaysia, MYA = Myanmar, PHI = Philippines, SIN = Singapore, THA = Thailand, VIE = Viet Nam.
Note: ASEAN-6 labeled in red, while CLMV in blue.
Source: Author estimates; World Bank. World Bank Open Data. https://data.worldbank.org/ (accessed 21 August 2022).

The terms θ and δ are member state and time effects, respectively. Member state effects represent all those economic characteristics of the member states that affect other determinants of economic growth and that we have not factored in $Z_{it}$. These effects can control for common shocks, such as climate change and spillovers across member states, which are difficult to model. Member state dummy variables can also be seen as an alternative to including country-specific fixed effects. The latter can exacerbate problems with measurement errors, particularly when these errors are not persistent, by throwing away all the between-country variation. When the member state and time effects θ and δ, respectively, are assumed to be zero, and there are no control variables $Z_{it}$ used in the model specification, the model is called unconditional Beta-convergence, as compared to the more general model called conditional Beta-convergence.

The parameter β is the rate at which member economies approach their steady state and, hence, represents the speed of convergence. Based on this value, the so-called half-life can be computed, i.e., the time span that is needed for current disparities to be halved. If the value of γ is restricted to 0, absolute convergence is assumed, while if it is freely estimated, conditional convergence is assumed. The same specification can be used to test the existence of a convergence process on other indicators, such as HDI. We show results of linear dynamic panel data models using determinants from 10 indicators in this report (Table 18). Panel allows to account for unobserved unit-specific heterogeneity and to model dynamic adjustment or feedback processes. Generalized method of moments (GMM) estimation is the predominant estimation technique for models with endogenous variables, in particular lagged dependent variables, when the time horizon is short. The control variables used represent nearly all the dimensions (the exception being the second dimension); these variables were chosen as they have the most data availability. Missing data for the control variables were imputed[14] for purposes of the econometric modeling.

---

[14] Imputations involved mere extrapolation with linear interpolation, or carrying forward or backward time series data, and in cases where member states had no data, estimation with panel regression models using explanatory variables chosen by classification and regression trees.

**Table 18: Regression Results**

| | Pooled Ordinary Least Squares | Fixed Effects Panel Regression | First Differenced GMM | System GMM |
|---|---|---|---|---|
| Log GDP per capita (t-1) | 0.9729* | 0.9323* | 0.9323* | 0.9766* |
| Test Log GDP per capita (t-1) = 1 | (0.0070) | (0.0178) | (0.0180) | (0.0066) |
| Human Development Index | 0.0993* | 0.2378 | 0.2378* | 0.0952* |
| | (0.0443) | (0.1531) | (0.0856) | (0.0429) |
| Unemployment Rate | 0.0011 | –0.0010 | –0.0010 | 0.0016* |
| | (0.0008) | (0.0014) | (0.0015) | (0.0008) |
| Commercial bank branches | –0.0015* | –0.0007 | –0.0007 | –0.0014* |
| (per 100,000 adults)) | (0.0005) | (0.0007) | (0.0007) | (0.0005) |
| Maternal Mortality Ratio | 0.0000 | –0.0001 | –0.0001 | –0.0001 |
| | (0.0000) | (0.0001) | (0.0001) | (0.0000) |
| Gross enrollment rate – | –0.0001 | 0.0002 | 0.0002 | –0.0003 |
| Preprimary | (0.0001) | (0.0002) | (0.0002) | (0.0001) |
| Individuals using the internet | 0.0002 | 0.0000 | 0.0000 | –0.0003* |
| (% of population) | (0.0001) | (0.0002) | (0.0002) | (0.0001) |
| Proportion of seats held by | –0.0002 | 0.0002 | 0.0002 | –0.0001 |
| women in national parliaments | (0.0003) | (0.0006) | (0.0007) | (0.0003) |
| (%) | | | | |
| Access of population to electricity | –0.0001 | 0.0000 | 0.0000 | –0.0007 |
| | (0.0002) | (0.0004) | (0.0004) | (0.0002) |
| Proportion of population covered | –0.0001 | 0.0002 | 0.0002 | 0.0002 |
| by social assistance programs | (0.0001) | (0.0002) | (0.0001) | (0.0001) |
| Ratio of protected area to total | 0.0001 | 0.0013 | 0.0013 | –0.0001 |
| area and forest cover to total | (0.0002) | (0.0011) | (0.0013) | (0.0002) |
| land area | | | | |
| Government Effectiveness Index | 0.0138* | –0.0050 | –0.0050 | 0.0164* |
| – Total | (0.0069) | (0.0125) | (0.0126) | (0.0066) |
| Constant | 0.2212 | 0.3635 | | 0.2652 |
| | (0.0400) | (0.1247) | | (0.0393) |

GDP = gross domestic product, GMM = generalized method of moments.
Note: * significant at 0.05.
Source: Author estimates.

The coefficients on the lagged dependent variable in all the models are found to have a value of less than 1 and to be statistically significant at the 5% level, providing strong evidence of conditional convergence. As expected, the magnitude of the coefficient for the lagged dependent variable estimated by ordinary least squares (OLS) is higher than that estimated using the fixed effects regression, and it is likely that the OLS estimate and fixed effects estimates give upward- and downward-biased estimates, respectively. The differenced GMM estimate for the lagged dependent variable is found to be the same as the fixed effects estimate. The empirical findings in this report partly validate results of Furuoka et al. (2018), which showed a positive causal relationship for 10% of two-country pairings of five ASEAN member states examined based on trade liberalization effects. Further, the findings here confirm the insights in several studies (e.g., Bucur and Stangaciu 2015, Jannset et al. 2016, Zulfiqar 2018, Bunnag 2019, Hrzic et al. 2020, Yaya et al. 2020), which point out that the development gap (among several Asian countries whether in terms of income or some other development indicator) declines over time conditional to controlling for several variables.

Sigma-convergence, on the other hand, means that all countries are converging to the same level of economic output per capita. If this is valid, we should then observe a falling variability of real (log) GDP per capita across ASEAN member economies over time. The latter can be explored by examining the trends in the coefficient of variation, i.e., the standard deviation divided by the mean, as a measure of dispersion, of GDP per capita among

ASEAN member states, and between CLMV versus ASEAN-6. The most frequently used summary measures of Sigma-convergence is the coefficient of variation (CV) of (log) GDP per capita for groups of countries, which is shown in Figure 16 for ASEAN-6 and CLMV for 2000 to 2021.

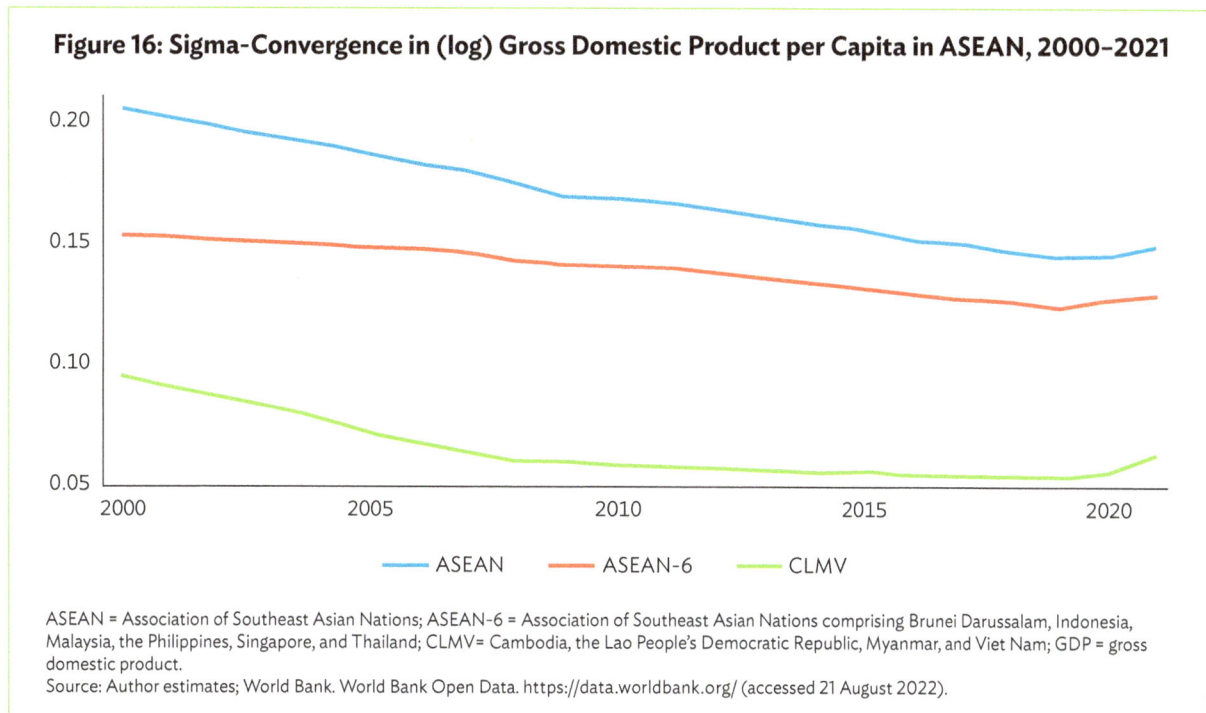

Figure 16: Sigma-Convergence in (log) Gross Domestic Product per Capita in ASEAN, 2000–2021

ASEAN = Association of Southeast Asian Nations; ASEAN-6 = Association of Southeast Asian Nations comprising Brunei Darussalam, Indonesia, Malaysia, the Philippines, Singapore, and Thailand; CLMV= Cambodia, the Lao People's Democratic Republic, Myanmar, and Viet Nam; GDP = gross domestic product.
Source: Author estimates; World Bank. World Bank Open Data. https://data.worldbank.org/ (accessed 21 August 2022).

The dynamics of income dispersion suggest that convergence in ASEAN was strong up to 2008 with the CV decreasing from 0.21 (in 2000) to 0.17 (in 2008). Since 2009, the CV has remained in a band of values between 0.15 and 0.17, with an uptick after the inception of the pandemic. Disparities within ASEAN-6 have not fallen as much as CLMV with the new member states in the ASEAN community catching up on the richest ones, at least before the pandemic, while among the richer member states that first joined the ASEAN, convergence has not been as rapid.

Sigma-convergence in ASEAN is further illustrated in historical data of the Gini index[15] calculated for the GDP per capita of ASEAN-6 and CLMV for 2000–2021 (Figure 17). The evolution of the Gini index on GDP per capita suggests that for ASEAN-6, the variability has not changed across the past 2 decades, while for CLMV, it has decreased, although amid the pandemic, the reverse of Sigma-convergence has resulted. To a large extent, the growth processes in ASEAN member states have had local differences, particularly in economic recovery. Overall, it appears that the slow convergence process within ASEAN-6 could be due, among other things, to some low degree of dispersion in per capita incomes, at least compared to CLMV.

Convergence analysis suggests that: (i) Beta-convergence processes have taken place among ASEAN member states, which means the poorest member states have been generating the fastest pace of economic performance, but this is the case only prior to the onset of the pandemic; (ii) ASEAN-6 did not show much Sigma-convergence, even prior to pandemic; and (iii) the pandemic halted whatever convergence processes and income leveling that was resulting, all things being equal.

---

[15] The Gini index is often used as a measure of inequality in the distribution of personal income. By definition, it varies between 0 and 1, with low values indicating more equal distribution (0 corresponding to perfect equality), while high values indicate more unequal distribution (1 corresponding to perfect inequality where income is concentrated in the hands of one individual). The Gini index here is used as an alternative measure of the variability of GDP per capita, i.e., to compare per capita GDP across different member states.

**Figure 17: Gini Index—Gross Domestic Product per Capita, ASEAN-6 and Cambodia, the Lao People's Democratic Republic, Myanmar, and Viet Nam, 2000–2021**

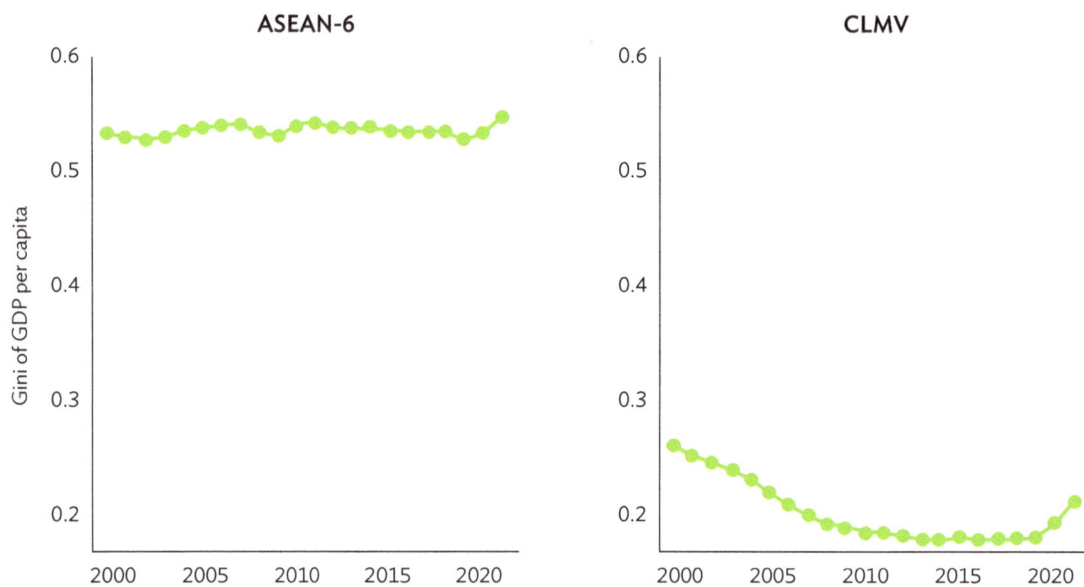

ASEAN-6 = Association of Southeast Asian Nations comprising Brunei Darussalam, Indonesia, Malaysia, the Philippines, Singapore, and Thailand; CLMV = Cambodia, the Lao People's Democratic Republic, Myanmar, and Viet Nam; GDP = gross domestic product.
Source: Author estimates; World Bank. World Bank Open Data. https://data.worldbank.org/ (accessed 21 August 2022).

# XV. WAYS FORWARD

Although this report provided an examination of a wealth of data on 39 development indicators across 12 dimensions of welfare, the analysis has been hindered by data issues, particularly the lack of disaggregated data. Development data are generally in the form of statistical aggregates, showing "big pictures." In contrast, disaggregated data, e.g., by gender, income, or age group, which are helpful to show disparities within countries, are of use for policies to yield equity and equality of opportunity. Discrimination, geography, governance, socioeconomic status, and shocks and fragility are among the major factors that can hide vulnerable groups across societies within aggregated data. These factors can also intersect, thus compounding the deprivations and reinforcing the limitations of marginalized people. However, disaggregated data are not always reported by national statistical systems (ADB 2021). Development data gaps persist in the region and across the world, either because of the frequency of conduct of data sources, or the lack of disaggregated data. Member states will need to make more investments to enhance the availability, quality, and disaggregation of data. Without sufficient development data, member states will be unable to set clear policy priorities, and the entire ASEAN community will not be able to develop an action agenda across countries, especially in promoting economic and social inclusion.

The discussions in this second AFEED Monitor point to many development issues, foremost of which is the need for increased investments in skills development by member states, and collectively by the ASEAN community. With the world influx from effects of various mega trends, resilience can only be developed among ASEAN peoples by developing their skills to cope with what the future brings. Benchmarking can be an effective way to narrowing development gaps, especially in skills. Benchmarks need to be periodically reviewed to assess progress in achieving targets, understand the barriers and bottlenecks to poor development performance, and identify issues that need critical attention, so that persisting inequalities within and across member states do not further widen (UNESCAP 2018a; 2018b; UNESCAP 2010).

As ASEAN member states tread on their paths of progress individually and collectively, the attention needs to shift from meeting basic targets to quality of life targets such as much improved skills in reading, math, and science; better nutrition; access to quality health care; and better evacuation centers in times of disasters. As the world has become digital, technology can widen inequality among and within ASEAN member states. People, firms, and countries that fail to invest in digital skills, infrastructure, and finance are likely to bear the costs of being less competitive.

The ASEAN community needs to invest in improving health and nutrition among its people. Productivity, particularly among the vulnerable groups, will increase if the young, especially, who are future workers, are better equipped physically, mentally, and emotionally. Food insecurity should be addressed, particularly in the wake of rising food prices that have had clear impacts on the poor and marginalized people. ASEAN should make sure that fortified foods are available especially for poor and vulnerable people. Instead of providing subsidies to consumers, governments can incentivize farmers to plant fortified grains and target the distribution of these to areas with high prevalence of malnutrition or hunger. The pandemic showed vulnerabilities of health systems in the ASEAN. It is important for member states to fortify health systems, including data systems for tracking diseases to improve resilience against future pandemics. Strengthening the monitoring and disease surveillance, particularly in highly populated areas and in remote rural areas, is crucial for ASEAN's health security. Investments in surveillance can be very effective not only in reducing deaths and diseases, but also in yielding faster economic recovery from pandemic effects.

While CLMV have made some headway in socioeconomic development especially prior to the pandemic, the gaps of CLMV with ASEAN-6 must be narrowed down, by way of more "ASEAN-help-ASEAN" projects. The Fourth Initiative for ASEAN Integration (IAI) workplan is a good plan that improves on previous workplans, but like all plans, it needs to have a clear results framework communicated to all stakeholders, and a means of effective implementation. The workplan aims to have better country ownership—it is critical to involve CLMV as early as during project development and include them also in the monitoring processes. The ASEAN Secretariat should work toward ensuring that the IAI workplan is aligned and mainstreamed within national development plans of all member states. Sustainable financing is also crucial given the many competing development priorities supported by the development community—stronger efforts must be made by the ASEAN Secretariat to collaborate with international organizations in finding critical resources for the IAI workplan implementation, including monitoring and evaluation.

A specific area of partnership of mutual benefit to CLMV and ASEAN-6 is on protecting the environment. Many development goals and targets, especially the SDGs, are mutually reinforcing. The eradication of extreme poverty can be achieved faster with investments in quality education and lifelong learning for all that can empower poor people and other vulnerable sectors to get better jobs.

The region has borne the brunt of climate change, especially climate-related hazards; thus, partnerships for climate action are not only necessary to address this "silent killer," but also provide new opportunities for innovation. It can be argued that meeting climate goals will help meet other socioeconomic goals and improve lives, particularly of those vulnerable to climate impacts. Using affordable, clean, and renewable energy will impact on health, education, productivity and environment, particularly in areas with high incidence of poverty. New technologies to store rainwater can also impact on health and productivity particularly of poor people, especially those living in urban areas.

Given the rapid urbanization in ASEAN, with majority of the population expected to live in urban areas by 2050, it is critical to develop urban agriculture, reduce and manage food waste, boost green spaces, develop more peri-urban areas, and reconnect cities with rural locales to make cities healthier and more sustainable. ASEAN also needs to monitor the quality of life in urban settings, aside from continuing its innovations in urban housing, transportation, and infrastructure. Access to cheap and clean energy, safe water, and sanitation are also needed on top of basic social services.

Innovation must also be harnessed in business processes and basic public service delivery across member states. More widespread digitalization and use of the internet can be mechanisms for wealth creation for all, especially those likely to be left behind. More affluent member states can provide technical assistance–especially to CLMV–for improving internet connectivity stability and access as well as enhancing digital skills, especially as some have become life skills, while others are needed at the workplace. Enhanced trade within ASEAN, not only in as far as goods and services but also in human resources, can harness sustainable consumption and production, aside from increasing economic opportunities, so that, ultimately, no person and no member state in the ASEAN community will be left behind.

# REFERENCES

Albert, J. R. G., M. R. M. Abrigo, F. M. A. Quimba, and J. F. V. Vizmanos. 2022. Poverty, the Middle Class, and Income Distribution amid COVID-19. *In The Philippines' Response to the COVID-19 Pandemic: Learning from Experience and Emerging Stronger to Future Shocks.* Book No. 2022-02: pp. 407–472. Manila: Philippine Institute for Development Studies. https://pidswebs.pids.gov.ph/CDN/document/pidsbk2022-covid19.pdf.3.

Alkire, S., and J. Foster. 2011. Counting and Multidimensional Poverty Measurement. *Journal of Public Economics.* 95(7–8): pp. 476–487. https://www.sciencedirect.com/science/article/abs/pii/S0047272710001660.

Alkire, S., U. Kanagaratnam, and N. Suppa. 2018. *The Global Multidimensional Poverty Index* (MPI): 2018 Revision. https://ophi.org.uk/wp-content/uploads/G-MPI_2018_2ed_web.pdf.

Asian Development Bank (ADB). Asian Development Bank: Key Indicators Database Online. https://kidb.adb.org.

_____. 2013. *Framework of Inclusive Growth Indicators 2012: Key Indicators for Asia and the Pacific, Special Supplement.* 3rd Edition. Manila. https://www.adb.org/publications/framework-inclusive-growth-indicators-2012-key-indicators-asia-and-pacific.

_____. 2021a. *Practical Guidebook on Data Disaggregation for the Sustainable Development Goals.* Manila. https://www.adb.org/sites/default/files/publication/698116/guidebook-data-disaggregation-sdgs.pdf.

_____. 2021b. *Learning and earning losses from COVID-19 school closures in developing Asia: Special Topic of the Asian Development Outlook 2021.* Manila. https://www.adb.org/sites/default/files/publication/692111/ado2021-special-topic.pdf.

_____. 2022a. The Social Protection Indicator for Asia: Tracking Developments in Social Protection. Manila. https://www.adb.org/sites/default/files/publication/849591/social-protection-indicator-asia-tracking-developments.pdf.

_____. 2022b. *Falling further behind: The cost of COVID-19 school closures by gender and wealth: Special Topic of the Asian Development Outlook 2021.* Manila.https://www.adb.org/sites/default/files/publication/784041/ado2022-learning-losses.pdf.

ADB and Association of Southeast Asian Nations (ASEAN) Secretariat. 2019. *Assessment of the Progress in Narrowing the Development Gap in ASEAN.* Jakarta: ASEAN Secretariat.

ADB Institute (ADBI). 2014. ASEAN 2030: *Toward a Borderless Economic Community.* Tokyo: ADBI. https://www.adb.org/sites/default/files/publication/159312/adbi-asean-2030-borderless-economic-community.pdf.

Association of Southeast Asian Nations (ASEAN) Secretariat. 2017. ASEAN *Community Progress Monitoring System.* Jakarta: ASEAN Secretariat. https://www.aseanstats.org/wp-content/uploads/2017/09/ACPMS_2017.pdf.

_____. 2019. *Regional Study on Informal Employment Statistics to Support Decent Work Promotion in ASEAN.* Jakarta: ASEAN Secretariat, December 2019. https://asean.org/asean2020/wp-content/uploads/2021/01/Regional-Study-on-Informal-Employment-Statistics-to-Support-Decent-Work-Promotion-in-ASEAN-2019.pdf.

_____. 2020a. *Mid Term Review of the ASEAN Socio Community Blueprint 2025.* (October) Jakarta: ASEAN Secretariat. https://asean.org/wp-content/uploads/2021/10/05-Full-Report-ASCC-MTR-Report.pdf.

_____. 2020b. *Mid-Term Review of Master Plan on ASEAN Connectivity 2025: Executive Summary*. (November). Jakarta: ASEAN Secretariat. https://asean.org/wp-content/uploads/2021/03/The-Mid-Term-Review-of-Master-Plan-on-Connectivity-MPAC-2025.pdf.

_____. 2020c. *ASEAN Rapid Assessment: The Impact of COVID-19 on Livelihoods Across ASEAN*. Jakarta: ASEAN Secretariat. https://asean.org/storage/ASEAN-Rapid-Assessment_Final-23112020.pdf.[JMPL1]

_____. 2020d. *ASEAN Sustainable Development Goals Indicators Baseline Report 2020*. Jakarta: ASEAN Secretariat. https://www.aseanstats.org/wp-content/uploads/2020/11/ASEAN-Sustainable-Development-Goals-Indicators-Baseline-Report-2020-web.pdf.

_____. 2020e. *ASEAN Key Figures 2020*. Jakarta: ASEAN Secretariat. https://www.aseanstats.org/wp-content/uploads/2020/11/ASEAN_Key_Figures_2020.pdf.

_____. 2020f. *Initiative for ASEAN Integration (IAI) Work Plan IV (2021-2025)*. (November) Jakarta: ASEAN Secretariat, November 2020. https://asean.org/wp-content/uploads/IAI-workplan-IV.pdf.

_____. 2021a. *2021 ASEAN Development Outlook: Inclusive and Sustainable Development*. (July). Jakarta: ASEAN Secretariat. https://asean.org/wp-content/uploads/2021/07/ASEAN-Development-Outlook-ADO_FINAL.pdf.

_____. 2021b. *Mid Term Review: ASEAN Economic Community Blueprint 2025*. (April). Jakarta: ASEAN Secretariat. https://asean.org/wp-content/uploads/2021/04/mid-term-review-report.pdf.

_____. 2021c. *ASEAN Digital Masterplan 2025*. Jakarta: ASEAN Secretariat https://asean.org/wp-content/uploads/2021/08/ASEAN-Digital-Masterplan-2025.pdf.

_____. 2022a. *ASEAN Digital Integration Index Report 2021: Measuring Digital Integration to Inform Economic Policies* (August). https://asean.org/wp-content/uploads/2021/09/ADII-Report-2021.pdf.

_____. 2022b. *ASEAN Economic Integration Brief*. Volume (June) Number 11. https://asean.org/wp-content/uploads/2022/06/AEIB_No.11-June-2022.pdf.

ASEAN Statistics Division. 2018. ASEANstats Database on SDG Indicators. https://data.aseanstats.org/sdg.

Atamanov, A., D. Jolliffe, C. Lakner, and E. B. Prydz. 2018. Purchasing Power Parities Used in Global Poverty Measurement. *Global Poverty Monitoring Technical Note* 5. Washington, DC: World Bank. https://documents1.worldbank.org/curated/en/764181537209197865/pdf/129965-WP-PUBLIC-Disclosed-9-19-2018.pdf?fbclid=IwAR2KOY0NfWVReubU103JDGM-JSRV0dehqxCRe5f9QFjpwGO9SrAsbaNGwFs.

Baird, S., F. H. G. Ferreira, B. Özler & M. Woolcock (2013). Relative Effectiveness of Conditional and Unconditional Cash Transfers for Schooling Outcomes in Developing Countries: A Systematic Review. Campbell Systematic Reviews, John Wiley & Sons, vol. 9(1), pages 1-124. https://onlinelibrary.wiley.com/doi/full/10.4073/csr.2013.8.

Barro, R. J. 1991. Economic Growth in a Cross Section of Countries. *The Quarterly Journal of Economics*. 106(2): pp. 407–443. https://doi.org/10.2307/2937943.

Behrman, J. A. 2015. The effect of increased primary schooling on adult women's HIV status in Malawi and Uganda: Universal Primary Education as a natural experiment. *Social Science & Medicine*. 127: pp. 108–115. ISSN 0277-9536. https://www.sciencedirect.com/science/article/pii/S027795361400402X.

Bucur, I.A., and O.A. Stangaciu. 2015. The European Union Convergence in Terms of Economic and Human Development. *CES Working Papers*. Volume VII. Issue 2. https://ceswp.uaic.ro/articles/CESWP2015_VII2_BUC.pdf.

Bunnag, S. 2019. Income and HDI Convergence in the Mekong Economies: Regional Development Revisited. Special Issue on Mekong Economy, the *Social Science Review, 2019*. Japan: Saitama University. https://core.ac.uk/download/pdf/210569451.pdf.

Cahyadi, N., R. Hanna, B. A. Olken, R. A. Prima, E. Satriawan, and E. Syamsulhakim. 2020. Cumulative Impacts of Conditional Cash Transfer Programs: Experimental Evidence from Indonesia. American Economic Journal: Economic Policy, 12 (4): 88-110. https://www.aeaweb.org/articles?id=10.1257/pol.20190245.

Department of Information and Communications Technology (DICT). 2019. National ICT Household Survey 2019. https://dict.gov.ph/ictstatistics/nicths2019/.

Furuoka, F., R. Rasiah, R. Idris, P. Ziegenhain, R. I. Jacob, and Q. Munir. 2018. Income Convergence in the Asean-5 Countries. *International Journal of Business and Society*. 19(3): pp. 554–569. http://www.ijbs. unimas.my/images/repository/pdf/Vol19-no3-paper1.pdf.

Hrzic, R., T. Vogt, F. Janssen, and H. Brand. 2020. Mortality Convergence in the Enlarged European Union: A Systematic Literature Review. *European Journal of Public Health*. 30(6): pp. 1108–1115. https://academic. oup.com/eurpub/article/30/6/1108/5811104.

ICF. 2012. The DHS Program STATcompiler. Funded by United States Agency for International Development (USAID). http://www.statcompiler.com.

International Monetary Fund (IMF). Financial Access Survey. https://data.imf.org/fas.

International Telecommunications Union (ITU). 2018. *Digital Skills Assessment Guidebook*. Geneva, Switzerland: ITU. https://www.itu.int/en/ITU-D/Digital-Inclusion/Documents/ITU%20Digital%20 Skills%20Toolkit.pdf.

_____. 2023. World Telecommunication/ICT Indicators Database. https://www.itu.int/en/ITU-D/Statistics/ Pages/publications/wtid.aspx.

Inter-Parliamentary Union. Historical Data on Women in National Parliaments. https://data.ipu.org/historical-women.

Islam, N. 2003. What Have We Learnt from the Convergence Debate. *Journal of Economic Surveys*. 17. pp. 309–362. Oxford, UK: Blackwell Publishing Ltd. USA. http://www.ecostat.unical.it/aiello/Didattica/ economia_Crescita/CRESCITA/islam_survey.pdf.

Janssen, F., A. van den Hende, J. de Beer, and L. van Wissen. 2016. Sigma and Beta Convergence in Regional Mortality: A Case Study of the Netherlands. *Demographic Research*. 35(4): pp. 81–116. https://www.demographic-research.org/volumes/vol35/4/35-4.pdf.

Jordá, V., & Sarabia, J. M. (2015). International Convergence in Well-Being Indicators. Social Indicators Research, 120(1), 1–27. http://www.jstor.org/stable/24721096.

Kovacevic, M., and M. C. Calderon. 2014. UNDP's Multidimensional Poverty Index: 2014 Specifications. *UNDP Human Development Report Office Occasional Paper*. https://hdr.undp.org/system/files/documents/ specificationsforcomputationofthempipdf.pdf.

Menon, J. 2013. Narrowing the development divide in ASEAN: the role of policy. *Asia-Pacific Economic Literature*. 27(2): pp. 25–51.

Molato-Gayares, R., A. Park, D. A. Raitzer, D. Suryadarma, M. Thomas, and P. Vandenberg. 2022. How to Recover Learning Losses from COVID-19 School Closures in Asia and the Pacific. *ADB Briefs*. No. 217. Manila: ADB. https://www.adb.org/sites/default/files/publication/808471/adb-brief-217-learning-losses-covid-19-school-closures.pdf.

Ryu, A. 4 Countries With Conditional Cash Transfer Programs. The Borgen Project. 23 November 2021. https://borgenproject.org/conditional-cash-transfer/.

Schwab, K. and S. Zahidi.  2020. Global competitiveness report: special edition 2020. World Economic Forum. https://www3.weforum.org/docs/WEF_TheGlobalCompetitivenessReport2020.pdf.

Social Progress Imperative. 2022. *The Social Progress Index Executive Summary*. https://www.socialprogress.org/st atic/9e62d6c031f30344f34683259839760d/2021%20Social%20Progress%20Index%20Executive%20 Summary-compressed_0.pdf.

Stiglitz, J., J. Fitoussi, and M. Durand. 2018. *Beyond GDP: Measuring What Counts for Economic and Social Performance.* Paris, France: OECD Publishing. https://doi.org/10.1787/9789264307292-en.

United Nations Department of Economic and Social Affairs. 2021. Sustainable Development Goals (SDG) Global Database. https://unstats.un.org/sdgs/dataportal.

United Nations Department of Economic and Social Affairs Population Division. 2022. *World Population Prospects 2022.* https://population.un.org/wpp/.

United Nations Development Programme (UNDP). Human Development Index. https://hdr.undp.org/data-center/human-development-index#/indicies/HDI.

_____. 1990. *Human Development Report.* New York: UNDP. http://hdr.undp.org/sites/default/files/reports/219/hdr_1990_en_complete_nostats.pdf.

_____. 2010. *Human Development Report: The Real Wealth of Nations: Pathways to Human Development.* New York: UNDP. https://hdr.undp.org/system/files/documents/human-development-report-2010-complete-english.human-development-report-2010-complete-english.

United Nations Economic and Social Commission for Asia and the Pacific (UNESCAP). 2010. *Striving Together ASEAN & the UN.* Bangkok: ESCAP. https://www.unescap.org/sites/default/files/Striving-Together-ASEAN-UN2010.pdf.

_____. 2018a. *Inequality in Asia and the Pacific in the Era of the 2030 Agenda for Sustainable Development.* Bangkok: ESCAP. https://www.unescap.org/sites/default/d8files/knowledge-products/ThemeStudyOnInequality.pdf.

_____. 2018b. *Subregional Perspectives on Inequality in Asia and the Pacific and Update on Subregional Activities for Development.* Item 3 (j) of the Provisional Agenda, Economic and Social Commission for Asia and the Pacific Seventy-fourth Session, Bangkok, 11–16 May 2018. https://www.unescap.org/sites/default/d8files/event-documents/E74_30E.pdf.

United Nations Educational, Scientific and Cultural Organization (UNESCO).1958. *Records of the General Conference Tenth Session.* Paris: UNESCO.

_____. 1978. *Records of the General Conference.* 20th session (vol. 1). Paris: UNESCO.

_____. 2014. *EFA Global Monitoring Report 2013/14: Teaching and Learning: Achieving Quality for All.* Paris: UNESCO.

_____. 2017. *Working Group on Education: Digital Skills for Life and Work.* Paris: UNESCO. https://unesdoc.unesco.org/ark:/48223/pf0000259013/PDF/259013eng.pdf.multi.

UNESCO Institute for Statistics. Data for the Sustainable Development Goals. http://uis.unesco.org/.

United Nations International Children's Emergency Fund (UNICEF), World Health Organization (WHO), and World Bank. 2021. The UNICEF/WHO/WB Joint Child Malnutrition Estimates (JME) group released new data for 2021. https://www.who.int/data/gho/data/indicators/indicator-details/GHO/gho-jme-country-children-aged-5-years-stunted-(-height-for-age--2-sd).

United Nations Women (2015). Unlocking the Lockdown: The Gendered Effects of COVID-19 on Achieving the SDGs in Asia and the Pacific.

UN Women Regional Office for Asia and the Pacific: Bangkok, Thailand. https://data.unwomen.org/sites/default/files/documents/COVID19/Unlocking_the_lockdown_UNWomen_2020.pdf.

World Bank. Learning Poverty Global Database: Historical Data And Sub-Components. https://datacatalog.worldbank.org/search/dataset/0038947.

_____. World Bank Open Data. https://data.worldbank.org/.

_____. Worldwide Governance Indicators. https://databank.worldbank.org/source/worldwide-governance-indicators.

_____. 2004. Doing Business Data. https://archive.doingbusiness.org/en/data.

_____. 2008. Global Purchasing Power Parities and Real Expenditures: 2005 International Comparison Program. Washington, DC. http://hdl.handle.net/10986/21558.

_____. 2013. Atlas of Social Protection: Indicators of Resilience and Equity (ASPIRE). World Bank: Washington, DC. https://www.worldbank.org/en/data/datatopics/aspire.

_____. 2014. *Bridging the Development Gap: ASEAN Equitable Development Monitor 2014.* (November). Washington, DC: World Bank. https://openknowledge.worldbank.org/bitstream/handle/10986/21749/957310WP0P148800Development0Monitor.pdf.

_____. 2018. *The State of Social Safety Nets 2018.* Washington, DC: World Bank. https://openknowledge.worldbank.org/bitstream/handle/10986/29115/9781464812545.pdf.

_____. 2021. The Global Findex Database 2021: Finanical Inclusion, Digital Payments, and Resilience in the Age of COVID-19. https://www.worldbank.org/en/publication/globalfindex.

_____. 2022. Poverty and Inequality Platform. World Bank Group. https://pip.worldbank.org/home.

World Economic Forum (WEF). 2021. The Global Gender Gap Report 2022. https://www.weforum.org/reports/global-gender-gap-report-2022.

Yaya, O.S., F. Furuoka, K.L. Pui, R.I. Jacob, and C.M. Ezeoke. 2020. Investigating Asian Regional Income Convergence Using Fourier Unit Root Test with Break. *International Economics.* 161. pp. 120–129. Amsterdam: Elsevier. https://www.sciencedirect.com/science/article/abs/pii/S2110701719302902.

Zulfiqar, K. 2018. An Analysis of Income Convergence Across Asian Countries. *Forman Journal of Economic Studies.* 14: pp. 125–141. https://prdb.pk/article/an-analysis-of-income-convergence-across-asian-countries-3162.

www.ingramcontent.com/pod-product-compliance
Lightning Source LLC
Chambersburg PA
CBHW042034220326

41599CB00045BA/7393